Designing With Nature

The Ecological Basis for Architectural Design

Ken Yeang

McGraw-Hill, Inc.

New York San Francisco Washington, D.C. Auckland Bogotá
Caracas Lisbon London Madrid Mexico City Milan
Montreal New Delhi San Juan Singapore
Sydney Tokyo Toronto

Library of Congress Cataloging-in-Publication Data

Yeang, Ken, date.
    Designing with nature : the ecological basis for architectural
design / Ken Yeang.
        p.   cm.
    Includes bibliographical references and index.
    ISBN 0-07-072317-6
    1. Architecture—Environmental aspects. I. Title.
NA2542.35.Y43   1995
720'.47—dc20   95-3233
                                          CIP

1 2 3 4 5 6 7 8 9 0 DOC/DOC 9 0 0 9 8 7 6 5

ISBN 0-07-072317-6

*The sponsoring editor for this book was Joel Stein, the editing supervisor was
Stephen M. Smith, and the production supervisor was Donald F. Schmidt.
It was set in Palatino by Estelita F. Green of McGraw-Hill's Professional Book
Group composition unit.*

Printed and bound by R. R. Donnelley & Sons Company.

McGraw-Hill books are available at special quantity discounts to use as
premiums and sales promotions, or for use in corporate training
programs. For more information, please write to the Director of Special
Sales, McGraw-Hill, Inc., 11 West 19th Street, New York, NY 10011. Or
contact your local bookstore.

 This book is printed on recycled, acid-free paper containing a
minimum of 50% recycled, de-inked fiber.

Contents

Preface

In 1971, I started work on ecological design as a research assistant in the Technical Research Division at Cambridge University under John Frazer and Alex Pike. Frazer and Pike were studying the feasibility of building an "autonomous house" (after Buckminster Fuller).

Early in my delving into the technical aspects of the project, it became evident that the proposition of an autonomous house was essentially an ecological one. Contending that the development and design of the systems for the building were technical in nature, I believed that the theoretical aspects of ecological design had to be addressed first. There were few or no precedents for this course of action at that time. Subsequently, with leave from Frazer and Pike in 1972, I embarked on a separate research program examining the wider theoretical aspects of the project.

In examining the theoretical aspects of ecological design, there is also a broader question regarding architecture: can it be theoretical? I believe yes and no. Theoretical propositions would appear not to be essential for most laypeople whose building needs and understanding tend to be pragmatic and, in some instances, aesthetically interpretive. However, if an architecture has a theory, it can contribute to legitimizing a deeper aesthetic, intellectual, and behavior-affecting role than simply having an enclosural function. Linder (1992)* contends that architectural theory can be perceived as an admirable endeavor to make architecture theoretical rather than a body of theory that is architectural. Being theoretical involves the architect in borrowing the techniques and disciplines of the scientist or the philosopher, and we have to be aware that architecture does not share many features with philosophy or science. Design is not a scientific endeavor alone; it combines both art and science and is probably one of the last true polymath jobs in today's industrial society (Jackson, 1993, p. 93).†

The theory of ecological design presented here applies to the latter perception: It is not an architectural theory but a body of theory that is architectural. Ecological design theory, by nature of the interconnected and holistic characteristics of the earth's ecosystems, affects all aspects of human activity that have an impact on the natural environment. Consequently, ecological design theory can include, besides architecture, such seemingly disparate fields as energy production, efficient utilization, waste recycling, and reutilization.

*Linder, M., "Architectural Theory Is No Discipline," in Whiteman, J., Kipnis, J., and Burdett, R. (eds.) (1992), *Strategies in Architectural Thinking*, MIT Press, Cambridge, MA.

†Jackson, T. (1993), *Turning Japanese*, HarperCollins, London, p. 93.

The propositions in this book being essentially theoretical, their adoption for a particular building design project involves value judgments such as the acceptable levels and ranges of ecological impacts, and an individual designer's own method and interpretive approach. The theory presented here needs further advancement through quantitative development and systemic testing by implementation. However, it is hoped that this material will start subsequent design approaches in the right direction. If it contributes to creating a sustainable future, the intentions of this project will be achieved.

Ken Yeang

1
Ecology and Design

Design and the Ecological Debate

Green architecture or *sustainable architecture* are simply different terms for designing with nature and designing in an environmentally responsible way. The increasing concern over the impairment of the earth's natural systems (i.e., the ecosystems within the biosphere) has elicited a variety of reactions from designers resulting in many views toward ecologically responsive design. Design in relation to the earth's ecological problems refers to the future and is therefore both prognostic and hypothetical. This is exemplified in the concept of *sustainability*, which is described as "meeting the needs of the present without compromising the ability of future generations to meet their own needs" (McDonough, 1992).

On the one hand, everyone is affected by the debate on these problems as they refer to the future; and on the other, it is difficult to form a clear and final judgment because in the last resort this might be proven wrong in the future.

1

Extreme attitudes are being taken. There are some who predict a "doomsday" future (e.g., Ehrlich and Ehrlich, 1970; Commoner, 1971; Meadows et al., 1972; Shiva, 1993); and there are others who would claim that one should have more faith in technology to solve environmental problems and more confidence in the adaptability of the biosphere and of humanity (Engensberger, 1974; Kahn, 1978; Vale and Vale, 1991b). The verification of these opposing views remains to be demonstrated. In addition to the two viewpoints, there are those who acknowledge that they do not know, but then draw the conclusion that more research is needed before any action is taken to resolve any environmental problem. Now, when this view is held by those concerned with the erection of the built environment, it provides an easy excuse for doing nothing when confronted with the environmental consequences of building.

However, in applied ecology and its related disciplines, there is a vast body of knowledge, which comprises preventive and corrective measures that could have been taken but in the majority of situations were not. While it can be commonly agreed that research must go on, it should also be acknowledged that many of the earth's ecological systems and processes are too complex to be quantified and represented in total. Architects, designers, engineers, and all those whose work affects the environment must make everyday design decisions and take action on the basis of the information that is presently available. It is thus vital that the present inadequate state of knowledge should not be used as a reason for the evasion of preventive or corrective action and the evasion of the responsibility for the environmental impact of building projects.

The significance of taking design action based on a proper understanding of ecological criteria is obvious. Design and planning decisions that are made at the present time not only have an immediate effect on human society, but also could influence the environmental quality for subsequent generations. However, assessment and guidelines for design should be provided on the basis of what is already known rather than on the ignorance or the exclusion of environmental considerations.

The Designer's Concept of the Environment and the Ecologist's Concept of the Environment

If we are to endeavor to design in an ecologically responsive and responsible way, we need a holistic and comprehensive approach to looking at building design. However, before we can proceed, we also need to appreciate some of the basic concepts of ecology, including the structure and function of ecosystems, specifically from the point of view of the designer. The intention here is to seek out those aspects of ecology that influence the design process, the design decisions, and the designed system itself. Previously, ecology and environmental biology have been little understood by designers, and in many cases, such a lack of understanding has led to extensive environmental damage that could have been adverted had the proper preventive measures been carried out initially.

An immediate apparent discrepancy lies in the difference between the designer's understanding of the environment and the ecologist's. We can distinguish the end product of our design process as a designed *system,* which is the primary object of our endeavor, from its *environment* (those parts of the external world which interact with it). The validity of any model of a system and of the description of the system that the model provides will depend not only upon the character of the model, but also upon the assumptions that we make about the system's environment and about the environment's interaction with the system. It follows that if the designer makes erroneous initial assumptions regarding the environment and the designed system, this will eventually result in some dissonance in the interface between the designed system and its environment.

The importance of the environment to the system that lies within it is readily apparent. For instance, with living systems, their environment and its stability play a vital role in their survival (Sears, 1956). Except for those special cases of systems which are completely isolated from the external world (e.g., in classical thermodynamics), every living system on earth is affected in some way by the state and stability of its environment. Every act of building changes the environment.

At present, many designers tend to wrongly conceive the environment and its state as simply a physical and spatial zone (i.e., as a site and geographical location) on which the designed system is erected. They are not fully aware of (or some prefer to ignore) the existing ecological and biological systems inherent in their project sites. Many of the current design approaches that claim to be "green" do not show a thorough understanding of the earth's ecosystems and their functioning (e.g., Vale and Vale, 1991a, b; etc.). In an ecological design approach, the concept of the environment has to be regarded as much more inclusive, encompassing not only the physical (inorganic) milieu of the building but also the biological (organic) milieu as well (Rowe, 1961; see Fig. 1-1). In most building projects, we often find that the architect or the designer has completely omitted any consideration of the biological components of the project site's ecosystem.

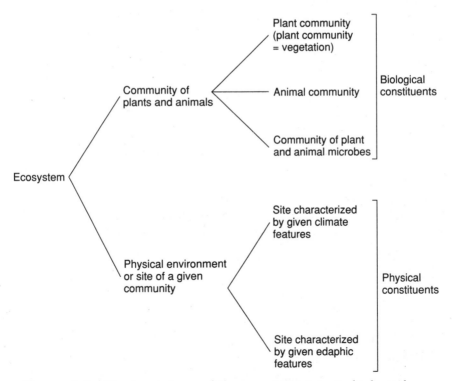

Figure 1-1. The breakdown of the ecosystem into its biological constituents and its physical constituents (adapted from Rowe, 1961).

To enable designers to appreciate the ecologist's concept of the environment, we need to first understand the ecologist's concept of the ecosystem, which is central to the study of ecology.

We can define *ecology* (a term originated by Haeckel in 1869) as the study of the interactions of organisms, populations, and biological species (including humans) with their living and nonliving environment; the composition change and stability of geographically localized groups of species, and the flow energy and matter within such groups of species (ecosystem) (Istock, 1973).

Ecologists contend that the interaction of both the biological and physical constituents of the environment together form a spatial unit, which is termed an ecosystem (Tansley, 1935). This ecological system or ecosystem is defined as a unit that includes all of the organisms (i.e., the community) in a given area, interacting with the physical environment, so that a flow of energy leads to a clearly defined trophic structure, biotic diversity, and material cycles (i.e., exchanges of materials between living and nonliving parts) within the system (Odum, E. P., 1971, p. 8).

In ecology, the term *ecosystem* is used both to define a unit of study and to describe a concept or an approach (McIntosh, 1963). For instance, as a *unit of study*, the term ecosystem can be applied to a unit of landscape or seascape for a definite segment of space and time (Van Dyne, 1969, p. 112). In a broader approach, the ecosystem *concept* provides a basis for examining environmental systems and their functioning.

The functions in the ecosystem include the transformation, circulation, and accumulation of matter and the

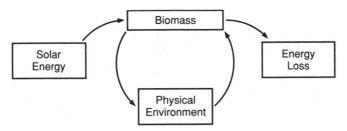

Figure 1-2. Circulation of energy.

flow of energy through the medium of living organisms and their activities and through natural processes (Van Dyne, 1969, p. 330; also see Fig. 1-2). The ecosystem's other functions include photosynthesis, herbivory, carnivory, and symbiosis (Van Dyne, 1966).

The main components that compose an ecosystem are (Odum, E. P., 1972):

- *Inorganic substances (carbon, nitrogen, carbon dioxide, water, etc.).* These substances are included in material cycles within the ecosystem.
- *Organic compounds (proteins, carbohydrates, etc.).* These compounds link biotic and abiotic substances.
- *Climate regime (temperature, rainfall, sunshine level, etc.).* The climate has an effect on which organisms can prosper in a given ecosystem.
- *Autotrophic organisms (producers).* These are mainly green plants that are able to manufacture food from simple substances. Autotrophic means "self-feeding."
- *Heterotrophic organisms (consumers).* These are mainly animals that ingest other organisms. Heterotrophic means "other feeding." There are three types of heterotrophic organisms:

- *Herbivores (primary consumers or "plant eaters").*
  Herbivores get their energy directly from plants.
- *Carnivores (secondary consumers or "meat eaters").*
  Carnivores get their energy from green plants
  by consuming herbivores.
- *Tertiary consumers.* Carnivores that feed on
  other carnivores.

- *Decomposers.* These are organisms like bacteria
  and fungi that break down complex substances
  into more elemental substances.

These factors indicate the complexities of our environment, which many designers tend to conveniently forget.

A close understanding of the ecosystem concept is
vital before we can relate a design to its environment. This is the first important aspect to an ecologically responsive approach to design. This means
that the ecosystem of the project site and its components must first be analyzed and studied holistically
so that we can thoroughly understand its components and processes (e.g., the energy transformations) and its susceptibility to change and design
intervention.

Simultaneously, in the ecological approach, our
designed system itself must also be analyzed. This
can be in the form of an intentional intrusion into
the project site's ecosystem in order to understand
and to anticipate the accompanying changes to its
structure and functioning caused by imposing a
man-made system upon it. However, the extent of
the impact of this intrusion will vary depending
upon other factors, such as the biological diversity
and stability of the project site, the geographical

location, the development history of the site, and the action inflicted. For example, a rural site will tend to be more ecologically diverse and complex (and thus more susceptible) than, say, an already cleared lot in a redeveloped urban area.

In many instances, it has been found that it is the designer's simplistic understanding of the ecology of our environment that has resulted in many of the present environmentally insensitive urban land-use patterns and the present state of progressive degradation of the environment. We must emphasize that an acceptance and understanding of the ecologist's concept of the environment is vital to any approach to the problems of environmental impairment and pollution (e.g., Tukey et al., 1965). Clearly, such an approach to design differs from the designer's traditional approach in that the project site will now have to be seen to be more than just a spatial zone. It is also a living and functioning ecosystem, and one whose components need to be considered holistically along with the interactions of all its processes.

Finite Limitations of the Use of the Earth's Ecosystems and Resources

Another premise that is crucial to ecological design is that there are finite limitations to human use of the earth's ecosystems and resources.

Ecosystems operate in the portion of the earth called the biosphere, which consists of the totality of all the milieus on the earth's mantle. We might describe this as the largest and the most nearly self-contained biological system on earth; it includes all the earth's living systems maintaining a steady-state system intermediate in the flow of energy between the high energy inputs of the sun and the thermal sink of space (Odum, E. P., 1969, p. 5). Within this biosphere, the flow of materials tends to be cyclic (Sjors, 1955). The fact that this flow has a cyclic pattern has broad design implications with regard to the use of materials in the built environment. An analogy can be drawn in which the use of materials in the built environment should ideally be cyclic as well. (See Chap. 5.)

The biogeochemical cycles in the biosphere include the circulation of chemical elements (e.g., carbon, hydrogen, oxygen, nitrogen, phosphorus) from the physical environment (e.g., Hasler et al., 1972). Also included in these cycles are the circulation of water (the hydrologic cycle), the very slow erosion and uplift of continents (the geologic cycle), the complementary processes of photosynthesis and respiration (the ecological cycle).

More important, the earth and the biosphere can be considered a "closed materials system" with a finite mass. The processes and phenomena acting upon it are in a continuous patterned motion, and ecologically we can conceive the earth as a unit.

This finiteness defines the limit to which human use of the earth's resources (the organic and inorganic) is restricted. Therefore, the totality of the interactions between the biotic and abiotic constituents of all the ecosystems within the biosphere (or the ecosphere, after Cole, 1958) and the finite quantities of the earth's energy and material resources is our ecological context and as such can be considered the final limiting factor in all design

activity. It follows that a rational use of these resources would be prudent since all design inevitably
takes place within their confines. This premise
implies that the designer needs to optimize and conserve use of the earth's resources if we are to ensure
their continued availability for future generations
(i.e., in a sustainable approach to design).

Natural and Man-made Environment

A difficulty occurs when examining the relationship
between the man-made and the natural environment, that is, is there a sharp distinction between
the "man-made" and the "natural" elements in the
environment? An example of this might be derelict
building land that has been recolonized by vegetation and animal life without any human intervention or management. In this example, the land has
been influenced both by people and by nature. This
difficulty in drawing a clear distinction is also
reflected in the many terms used to describe the
forms of vegetation succession encountered in terrestrial ecosystems (Tansley, 1935; Clements, 1946;
Philips, 1968).

Neither the word *natural* nor the word *man-made*
is entirely satisfactory since people are a part of
nature as a biotic component and all communities,
whether strongly influenced by humans or not, are
also part of nature. However, because of humanity's
pervasive influence, no area can be completely isolated from its direct or indirect effects. No part of
the earth could be termed to be completely natural;

some human modification of the environment has occurred, if no more than a minor change caused by chemical fallout from air pollution.

Some ecologists assert that the natural biological communities consist of naturally occurring species of flora and fauna that are able to maintain themselves and their abiotic environment in the absence of humans. Man-made communities are those characterized by species introduced by humans or favored by human modifications that are unable to exist without continued human assistance or interference, e.g., gardens and agricultural systems (Duffey and Watt, 1970). Though it is useful to distinguish them for some purposes, both categories always exist as part of the biosphere. Simultaneously, it is helpful to conceive of the situation in a way that visualizes the interactive subparts and individual components (Angyal, 1941). Our distinction here between man-made and natural is synthetic and primarily intended for analytical purposes. People are therefore considered to be part of a closed system and part of the processes of the natural environment, which being unitary must be considered an important factor in influencing and limiting human's activities upon the earth.

The Spatial Interaction between Ecosystems

The next premise of design is that the impact of a design is not restricted to its site's legal boundaries. Many designers tend to delineate their project sites as discrete areas which are isolated from other areas by fences, walls, and boundary lines. However, in the biosphere, ecosystems are not isolated systems but have a spatial interlocking property, which is characterized by their parts and by the interactions among the parts (Dasman, 1972). The interactions between ecosystems extend across artificial man-made boundaries.[1] Ecosystems in the biosphere must be seen holistically as interdependent. One of the most important elements of ecological thought is this emphasis on a holistic approach (McIntosh, 1963; Billings, 1964; Boughey, 1971; Egler, 1972) which is incorporated in the ecosystem concept (Tansley, 1935). There is a web of interdependencies and relationships within and between ecosystems, such that changes to any one part of the system will affect the operation of the whole (in the immediate or long-term sense), even though the precise degree of interdependence may seem remote (Arvil, 1970; Williams and House, 1974).

From this, it follows that the designer must conceive the project site in its larger geographical context as part of its ecosystem unit that is defined by natural boundaries. Because of the complexity and the inseparability of the interactions between ecosystems and within an ecosystem, the designer must not take a fragmented view of an ecosystem, that is, to look at only one isolated spatial segment or component of the ecosystem. For instance, by concentrating on one fragment and trying to optimize the performance of that fragment, it is likely that the rest of the system would respond in unsuspecting ways (Holling and Golberg, 1971). Further-

[1]We should note that even though physical structure can obstruct migration routes, other ecosystem interactions take place.

more, any human action on an ecosystem might influence not only its immediate environment but also the systems surrounding it and others within the biosphere. The ecological approach is therefore an environmentally holistic one.

The importance of this premise for design is readily apparent. For instance, many of the existing methods of pollution control claim to eliminate the contaminants, but in fact they merely alter the contaminants from one form to another form that is more expedient (e.g., financially expedient). Protective legislation relating to water pollution usually says nothing about air pollution or about the disposal of solid waste (land pollution). Thus, the local authority that is responsible for the protection of water courses is obliged by the legislation and by economic expediency to transfer the contamination problems from one environmental zone to another, regardless of their effects.

A holistic approach to design requires a proper understanding of the spatial interactions of ecosystems. In some cases the environment for the building project has been wrongly conceived by the designer as consisting of isolated and discrete environmental zones such as *land, air, water,* etc. (see Fig. 1-3). Such a model of the environment is simplistic and may lead to unanticipated and undesirable effects (Spofford,

| Land | Air | Water | Others |

Figure 1-3. Environmental zones. Some environmentalists wrongly conceive the environment in terms of discrete zones which do not interact with one another.

1973). Although it may sometimes be convenient to consider the environment horizontally in terms of "layers" (i.e., lithosphere, hydrosphere, biosphere, and atmosphere), we should be aware that these layers are not mutually exclusive but are spatially interfused by the various ecological processes and interdependencies. In order to anticipate the effect of any action on an ecosystem, a synoptic understanding of the interaction among its components is needed (e.g., Van Dyne, 1969) (see Fig. 1-4).

In site planning for the built environment, the designer must therefore be aware that any structure which he or she locates upon a project site will inevitably, by virtue of its physical presence and functioning, affect not only that site's ecosystem but others elsewhere (e.g., the air pollution discharged from the building's mechanical systems can be transferred regionally by the biosphere's atmospheric

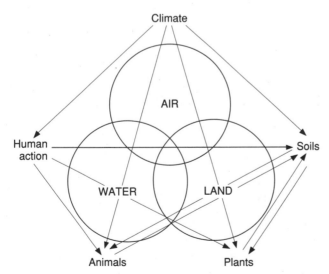

Figure 1-4. The three layers of air, water, and land and the interaction of the biotic factors.

process). The structure's possible influences on surrounding ecosystems and other ecosystems in the biosphere must be included as part of the set of design considerations.

The Dynamic State of the Ecosystem and Its Changing Interactions with the Built Environment over Time

Having described the ecosystem concept and the components, we must now consider the interaction of these over time. Ecologists contend that the environment is in a dynamic state and is therefore in a continuous state of flux. The biosphere and the ecosystems within it must not be regarded as being in a static, timeless, or primeval condition (LaPorte et al., 1972), since environmental processes (such as the normal geologic actions of erosion and sedimentation or the shifting of climates and habitats) have kept the whole biospheric system in a state of flux throughout geological time (Flawn, 1970). This being the case, then, all the systems within the biosphere are dynamic systems, and their relationships are therefore continuously changing and modifying over time (e.g., seasonal change within ecosystems). It follows that for all built environments there is a continuously changing and dynamic state of interaction between people and built systems; between built systems and their infrastructures; between these infrastructures and the ecosystems of the project site; and between these ecosystems and other ecosystems in the biosphere.

In design terms, we cannot regard the built environment as a static and immutable system which has negligible or unchanging interactions with the ecological systems. After a built system has been located, constructed, and put into operation, it will continue to interact with the environment over its entire physical life span. In the ecological approach, the designer needs to predict and to monitor the range of environmental interactions and consequences of the design not only prior to its construction, but also during its operation and use. The present scope of the designer's responsibilities now needs to include responsibilities for things such as the disposal of the components of the built system at the end of their useful life. In many instances, the ecological consequences of a built system during its period of use and operation exceed by far the consequences incurred in its initial realization (e.g., through its high consumption of energy and emissions of waste and other discharges). Ecological design should therefore involve a total and holistic approach to the energy and material resources management of built elements. In order to do so, it is useful to consider every built system conceptually as a designed system that has its own life-cycle pattern. (See Chap. 5.)

Traditionally, the architect has been responsible for the assembly of materials at the site, the construction of the building, and often the maintenance and renovation of the building after it has been completed. However, an ecological design approach would require that the designer be concerned not only with these traditional responsibilities but also with the ecological interactions between the designed system and its environment over its entire physical life cycle.[2] This would, in effect, entail an examination of the projected flow of materials and energy used during the life cycle of the built environment and the possible routes that they might take from their source to their sink, along with a system for monitoring by the designer the changes that take place in ecosystems over that period.

In this way, we might even redefine architectural design as a form of energy and materials management, where the earth's energy and material resources are managed and assembled by the designer into a temporary form (viz., for the period of use), and then demolished at the end of the period of use, with the materials either recycled within the built environment or assimilated into the natural environment.

The Spatial Heterogeneity of Ecosystems

Ecosystems possess a spatial heterogeneity which includes differences in biological and physical properties in space and time. This means that the extent of impact and the risk of permanent degradation to the ecology of any locality posed by human action or activity varies depending on the geographical locality and on the type of human action and activity imposed on it.

Spatial heterogeneity represents a mosaic of patches that are either temporally out of phase with each other or quantitatively different in biological composition. For instance, the various flora and fauna in

[2]While this cannot be absolutely done in practice, the principle of total responsibility is a necessary objective.

ecosystems are not located haphazardly over the surface of the earth; each species has a geographical range (Ehrenfield, 1970, p. 40), where the primary determinants of the distribution of species are generally geology (bedrock and drift) and climate. These factors account for other variables, such as the pattern and distribution of soils, topography, water regimen, yearly temperature profile and rainfall, and the distribution of other species. To these variables are added the extent of human action and activity already inflicted on that locality. In the same way that no two biological species are exactly the same, no two localities can be deemed totally similar in ecosystem properties.

Previously, designers have approached ecosystems as merely physical sites on which their acts of transformation take place; ecosystems have been viewed as elements to be modified and shaped to suit the design. In the ecological approach, locations or project sites must not be regarded by the designer as uniform, even though superficially one may appear similar to others. Each project site needs to be individually evaluated, with consideration given to the ecosystem's own natural values, its processes, its constraints, and its inherent array of natural opportunities, all of which differ with different locations (McHarg, 1968).

Spatial Displacement of Ecosystems by the Built Environment

The presence of any man-made structure (particularly a building) on an ecosystem creates conflicts with the ecosystem. For instance, its presence may increase soil erosion, alter the runoff of rainwater, modify the speed and direction of air flow, and change the way in which the sun's heat is absorbed and reflected. We do not mean that all of human actions have destructive consequences on ecosystems. Nevertheless, the built environment has effects over a specific segment of space and time. By its physical presence, the built environment, no matter how well designed, will intrude upon, displace spatially, and alter the ecology of the ecosystem on which it is located.

In addition to this spatial displacement in the ecosystem, most man-made structures and buildings result in a substantial physical introduction of energy and materials to the ecosystem of the project site. This is because all building activity involves a redistribution and a concentration of some portions of the earth's energy and material resources from usually distant locations to a specific locality (the project site), with the end result of changing the composition of that part of the earth's biosphere as well as adding to the composition of that ecosystem.

We can conceive an ecosystem prior to such human intrusion as an energy web in some relative state of stability (Odum, H. T., 1972). Then, as the result of building activity where excessive amounts of energy and material resources are brought in from different sources, the balance between the ecosystem's inputs and outputs of materials and energy is upset, and consequently its environmental web becomes warped and its biological structure becomes modified (see Figs. 1-5 and 1-6).

For example, the construction of a building on a

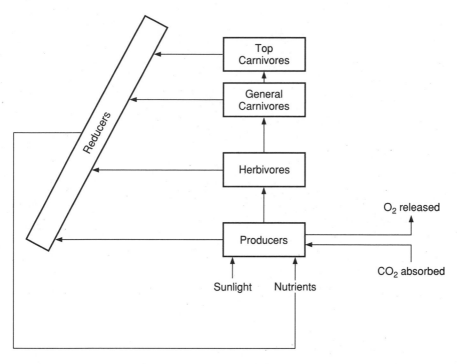

Figure 1-5. The cycling of materials within an ecosystem (adapted from Boughey, 1971).

green-field site involves the intentional and direct destruction of the physical and biotic substrate of the site. Usually the ground cover, shrubs, stumps, and trees within the building area are removed completely, up to some distance outside the building line. Then excavation to the required depth and size for the foundations and piling takes place. In the process of excavation, rainfall may increase the erosion of the topsoil and the sedimentation of nearby water bodies. Surrounding the built system, the biota and soil are often stripped away and replaced, usually by an impermeable (concrete, paved, or asphalt) surface. These surfaces decrease the perco-

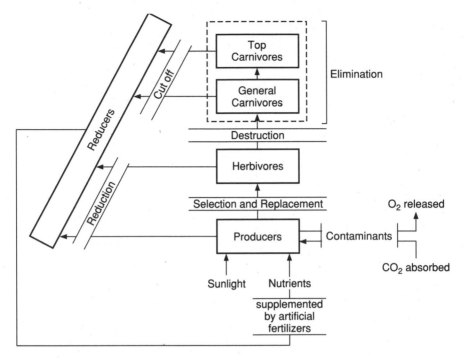

Figure 1-6. The range of possible dislocations to the ecosystem resulting from human intervention (adapted from Boughey, 1971).

lation of rainwater and increase the runoff, which may cause degradation to ecosystems elsewhere. The entire structure and functioning of the location's ecosystems are often affected (Yeang, 1972).

The ecosystem itself may offer certain natural opportunities that could be used. Vegetation cover can help to reduce temperature extremes, filter dust, break up winds, and maintain a desirable level of humidity in the local environment. However, in some intensely urbanized areas, only the climate component of the original ecosystem remains, and even this is modified by the different heat budgets of building materials (e.g., concrete and brick); the exhaust heat from heating and cooling systems; the greatly increased runoff from roofs and paved areas; and the smoke and fumes from industrial, domestic, and automobile sources. Other dependent cycles that maintain the global oxygen/carbon dioxide ratio in the ecosystem may be affected by the discharge of contaminants into the atmosphere or hydrosphere. These changes not only interfere with the ecosystem, they also give rise to secondary conflicts by their spatial juxtaposition with other human activities, which may subsequently impair their operation. When additional physical and biotic elements are introduced into the locality, the composition of the ecosystem is further modified.

Broadly stated, the common pattern in the deterioration of organic life as a result of building intrusion (both in the terrestrial and aquatic ecosystems) includes a decline in the biomass (the mass of living matter), a decline in productivity (the amount of material produced by a given species present in a given area), and the malfunctioning of natural controls (Woodwell, 1971).

Because the reproductive capacity of most plants and animals is relatively high, there can be a certain amount of recovery of vegetation and animal life in most ecosystems, if the damage has not been severe or if the total displacement of the ecosystem by the built system has been confined to relatively small areas. Usually, however, removal of the biota will result in a somewhat different flora and fauna population because there may be local extinction of certain species or genotypes (Billings, 1964). In addition, fluctuation in climatic cycles (e.g., temperature increase) causes unfavorable growing conditions for some kinds of organisms that were part of the preexisting ecosystem (prior to human intervention and modification). Species of flora and fauna vary in their genetic (heritable) properties over their geographical range (Krebs, 1972, Chap. 8). These genetic variations are the basis for the local adaptation of species to varying environments. However, a continued removal of "natural" or "seminatural" communities, say, over a continent (e.g., as a result of urban expansion), will eventually eliminate this resource and make effective rehabilitation with native species assemblages increasingly difficult. The act of clearing land for building purposes particularly contributes to the loss of such resources (Istock, 1973). It might be said generally that land that has been urbanized has the least potential for revegetation, even though some recolonization by hardier species or some rehabilitation with human help could be established (Dunn and Hington, 1970). However, in most cases, the ecosystem will suffer some deterioration and loss (Hutchinson, 1974).

This broad description of the effects of construction activity and human action on ecosystems is representative of the type of impairment that could take place in the project site's ecosystem. Any built environment, no matter how well designed, will have an impact (to a greater or lesser extent) on the locality on which it is sited by virtue of its spatial displacement of and its addition to the ecosystem. In the ecological approach, it is essential to ensure, by means of siting and layout of the built system in relation to the biotic and abiotic constituents of the ecosystem of that location, that the negative effects caused by the spatial displacement of the ecosystem are kept to a minimum. In addition to this consideration, the designer must be aware that the built system's own structure and mechanical systems constitute a substantial addition of materials, energy, and other biotic elements as well as human population to that ecosystem. In the ecological approach, the designer would need to ensure that these additions will not interact detrimentally with the ecosystem. In some instances, it may be that as a result of ecological analyses, the designer concludes that an alternative site should be selected instead of the one proposed.

Complexity of Impacts: Modifications to the Ecosystem Result in Multiple Effects

A basic difficulty in the construction (and refutation) of ecological hypotheses is that the effects of human modifications of ecosystems do not take place serially but in close interdependence. This is similarly true of attempts to seek solutions to single environmental problems (e.g., crises caused by the accidental contamination of an ecosystem by industrial effluents or oil spills). In pollution control, often, if not always, the corrective measures that are taken to control one critical factor lead to another getting out of control. It is a characteristic of ecosystems that they operate as nonlinear systems and cannot be characterized by a single, direct cause-and-effect relationship (Margalef, 1963). In the ecological approach, the designer needs to be aware that the interactions within an ecosystem and between ecosystems are complex functions and that ecosystems are fragile systems.

The actual interaction relationship might be more correctly described as a "cause-condition-effect" network (Sorenson, 1972; Sorenson and Moss, 1973). This means that a given action could cause one or more changes in the condition, which in turn can produce one or more subsequent condition changes before resulting in other effects acting holistically (see Fig. 1-7). For example, in building construction, the earthworks cut-and-fill and road-formation work on a site can cause erosion of soil slopes into the adjoining water streams. This will subsequently increase the stream turbidity, leading to shoaling of water courses or alteration of the stream channel. These in turn would increase the stream flood potential and block up the passage of the aquatic biota (by silta-

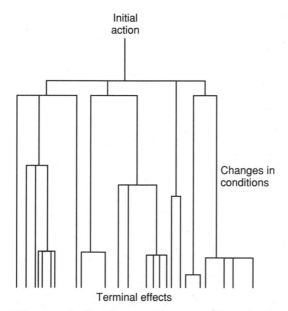

Figure 1-7. The escalating and multiple changes to the existing conditions that could take place as a result of a single action.

tion). All the components of the ecosystem are therefore physically and functionally interdependent. In some cases, the secondary and other orders of induced effects may be more damaging than the primary effects. In other cases, the sum of the effects may act synergistically to produce effects which are different quantitatively from the effects expected separately (Ray, 1970).

In the ecological approach, there is no single "technological fix" or universal design approach that will solve all environmental problems or eliminate all negative effects. It is not always possible to perform just one action in an ecosystem because the effects of one activity designed to accomplish a single purpose are in fact multiple.

While it is not always possible to predict all the multiple effects that could take place, the designer's responsibility is to be aware of and anticipate the consequences as far as possible early in the design stage. The ecological approach to design cannot be a simplistic single-purpose approach. The extent of anticipation of the impact of the design on the ecosystem will depend on the complexity of the individual project and the ecological value of the ecosystem in question.

In order to minimize undesirable impacts, the designer must comprehend and inventory the complex processes of the components of the ecosystem before the implementation of the designed system, and then attempt to predict at the design stage (insofar as possible) the effects on the ecosystem of each individual activity related to the construction of the designed system. An anticipatory design approach is again emphasized. Ideally, this must extend to anticipation of the effects of the range of activities during the operation of the designed system after it has been constructed and even after its useful life (i.e., throughout the designed system's entire life cycle).

Self-Regulation and Assimilative Ability of Ecosystems

Historically, the man-made environment has changed as a result of continued and extensive urbanization and land use, from being the contained system to the containing one (see Fig. 1-8) (after Chermayeff and Tzonis, 1971). In effect, the ecosystems in the biosphere are becoming increasingly saturated with man-made systems. This process of saturation has the overall effect of reducing regionally and globally the self-regulative and assimilative ability of the ecosystems. Broadly stated, human impacts on the ecosystem usually result in some degree of simplification— that is, from a diversified state to a less complex state. Often this results in reducing the flexibility of the relationship between the man-made environment and the ecosystem, while simultaneously increasing the ecosystem's constraints on the man-made environment. The overall effect is that people and their built systems have become not less dependent upon the functioning of the ecosystems within the biosphere, but, on the contrary, more dependent.

Since every designed system inevitably interacts with the environment, each will have a role in the earth's ecological systems, to a greater or lesser extent. However, over time, as the ecosystem's con-

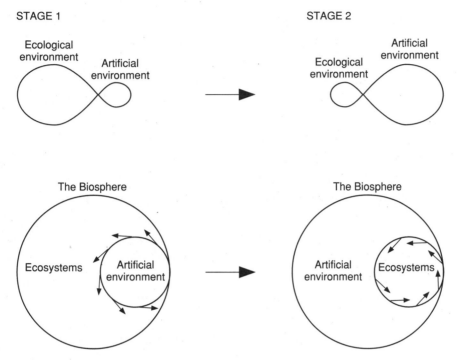

Figure 1-8. Biosphere saturation. The present man-made environment has changed from being a contained system to the containing system where the biosphere becomes increasingly saturated with man-made elements (after Chermayeff and Tzonis, 1971).

straints continue to become greater, this role of the designed system will become even more critical. The significance of this has not been fully realized by many designers. To the contrary, there are some designers who maintain that the ecosystem's capacity for absorption of impacts is tenacious enough that as people alter the ecosystem, they will be able to maintain it, by creating artificial subsystems to replace the natural ones on which they have previously depended. These designers further hold that in this way, technology can "keep ahead" of nature until eventually people will be able to become com-

pletely independent of the natural order by technological means (e.g., Landers, 1969). For example, this
mechanistic approach is reflected in some of the
designs for the built environment's life-support systems which have artificial controls (commonly
termed "controlled environments") where all the
existing self-regulating mechanisms of the ecosystem are replaced by externally regulated man-made
mechanisms (the mechanical systems for heating,
cooling, ventilation, illumination, waste disposal,
etc.). However, such a systemic control has the dis-
advantage of rendering the interaction between
man-made systems and the natural systems totally
dependent upon human efforts alone (Goldsmith,
1970). When man-made systems replace natural
ones, they generally are a gross simplification of
complex natural systems and consequently are particularly vulnerable to breakdown and failure.

As the assimilative ability of the ecosystem continues to be reduced, there must be an obvious limit
to the extent to which external man-made controls
may be permitted to replace the complex, ecologically self-regulating ones. There is therefore a limit
to which the man-made environment can be
allowed to replace and simplify the ecosystem. With
the present built environment, people have created
a situation where they must now return to the natural ecological controls, develop new ones, or
design some new combination. At present, it seems
unlikely that people can construct adequate artificial
control systems out of engineering hardware only,
while at the same time completely ignoring the natural ecological systems. The design options are
designing to integrate man-made designed systems

with ecosystems in such a way as to make use of existing natural controls and/or combining both man-made and ecosystem control structures.

In the ecological approach, the designer must appreciate that although an ecosystem is able to assimilate a certain amount of impairment to its processes, it has a definite limit to its assimilative ability. If an ecosystem is not to be permanently impaired, the designers must ensure that all the actions and activities that take place on it remain subject to the limitations inherent in the ecosystem and its components. In most instances, these limitations become apparent only after a proper examination of the ecosystem of the project site and its properties has been undertaken.

Human Acceleration of Entropy on the Earth

Briefly stated, entropy represents the extent to which the universe runs down during every natural process. This attribute can be thought of as the degree of dissipation within a system of the energy or force that enables the system to undertake work, whether this is internal dissipation or an export to the environment (Walmsley, 1972). Entropy can also be conceived as the degree of dilution or disorder in a system. It increases in every natural process (Berry, 1972).

As a consequence of their present and past demands on the earth's resources and ecosystems, people have short-circuited many of the biosphere's natural processes and accelerated the entropy increase in the biosphere. For example, central to the use of energy in the present built environment is the carbon cycle (in the use of fossil fuels). Human intervention of energy has short-circuited one of the biogeochemical cycles in the biosphere by simply speeding up one step in this cycle faster than the ability of the biosphere to regenerate this energy naturally (see Fig. 1-9). Similarly, it has been found

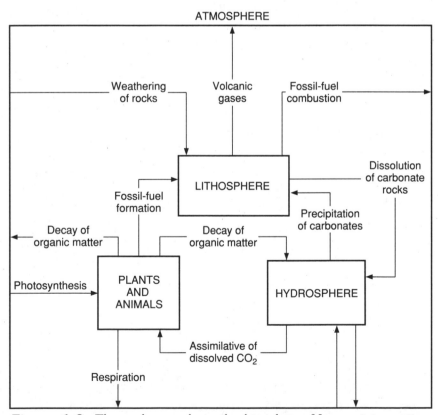

Figure 1-9. The carbon cycle in the biosphere. Human intervention through fossil-fuel combustion has accelerated one step in this cycle faster than the biosphere is able to regenerate naturally.

that other elements, such as iron, nitrogen, copper, zinc, lead, phosphorus, mercury, and tin, have also been mobilized in the biosphere by people in greater quantities than by nature (Bowen, 1972; Holdren and Ehrlich, 1974) through the extensive use of these material resources in the built environment (see Fig. 1-10).

However, there are some designers who contend that architecture, by its nature of ordering, averts the effects of entropy in the biosphere, and that this is in fact the purpose of design: to create order from chaos. In effect, that is an oversimplification of the role of architecture (Bertalanffy, 1968). Certainly entropy cannot but increase in an open system. In certain circumstances a living organism (an open system) feeds on negative entropy. It imports complex organic molecules, uses their energy, and then returns simpler end products to the environment. A

Element	Geological rate (river flow)	Human rate (mining and consumption)
Iron	25,000	319,000
Nitrogen	3,500	30,000
Copper	375	4,460
Zinc	370	3,930
Nickel	300	358
Lead	180	2,330
Phosphorus	180	6,500
Mercury	3	7
Tin	1.5	166

Figure 1-10. Humankind's mobilization of materials (10 metric tons/an): Comparison of geological rates with human consumption rates (from Holdren and Ehrlich, 1974).

living organism maintains itself in a steady state by importing materials that are rich in free energy, and thus, unlike a closed system, it avoids an increase in entropy. Nevertheless, some of its internal reactions will produce an increase in entropy. If we take the environment and the system into account holistically, then the total exchange of energy will always conform to the second law of thermodynamics. Seen in isolation, the living system itself will tend toward a higher state of order, differentiation, and complexity, but at the expense of energy won by oxidation and other energy-yielding processes. Other processes like growth, decay, and death represent approaches to and slow exchanges within a steady state, and each requires the expenditure of energy. The second law of thermodynamics is therefore not violated when entropy is considered in relation to the combined system and environment. This fact further emphasizes the holistic ecosystem approach to both the designed system and its environment.

The Bases for Ecological Design

Some of the fundamental premises which are crucial to the rationale for our ecological approach to design are as follows:

1. *The ecological concept of the environment.* In considering the project site, the designer needs to expand his or her previously restricted concept of the environment to incorporate the ecologist's concept of the environment. The ecologist contends that,

first, the environment of any built system must be seen in the overall context of the ecosystem unit on which this built system is located, and second, it also exists within the context of other ecosystems on the earth. If we apply the ecosystem concept to design, then the project site must at the outset be conceived holistically by the designer as a unit consisting of both its biotic and abiotic (living and nonliving) components functioning together as a whole to form an ecosystem, and before any human action can be inflicted on the project site, its features and interactions must be identified and fully understood.

For example, at present we find that the designer tends to examine mainly the physical features of the locality in which he or she proposes to locate the designed system. Such a site analysis is usually intended to provide the designer with a basis for determining, for instance, the best location for the designed system, the layout pattern and vehicular access, and the height and form of the designed system. However, in addition to these criteria, we would need an understanding of the project site's ecosystem to help the designer in determining the type and extent of human intervention that could be permitted for that ecosystem. The design task becomes one of integrating the designed system's features, processes, and functioning with the ecosystem's own processes and functioning in order to minimize the undesirable impacts and achieve a steady-state relationship with the ecosystem.

For instance, in designing the relationship between the designed system and its environment, we can identify three strategies: The designer can attempt to control the ecosystem processes (e.g., by

constructing a dam across a river to control floods),
succumb to them (e.g., by accepting the flood conditions and moving off the flood plain altogether), or
cooperate with them (e.g., by adjusting the flood
plain occupancy to the perceived flood intensity and
frequency and protecting those structures that are
still susceptible to the flood hazard). In the last case,
the constraints, restraints, and inherent opportunities of the ecosystem have to be examined closely in
the initial stages of design, after which design
efforts have to be based on the understanding of the
ecosystem and on the seeking of compatible combinations and interactions between the designed system and the ecosystem.

2. *Energy, materials, and ecosystem conservation
through design.* Because the earth is a closed materials system with a finite mass, all the ecosystems
within it, along with all of the earth's material and
fossil energy resources, form the final contextual
limit to all design activity. All design activity
inevitably takes place within the confines of this
limit. In an ecological approach to design, a more
rational use of ecosystems and resources is needed.
In the past, designers have erroneously conceived
the environment as an infinite source of all
resources and an infinite sink for all discharges and
waste products; in the ecological approach, the
designer needs to be specifically conscious of the
environment's limitations.

A rational approach to the use of the earth's
ecosystems, energy, and material resources means a
conservation-conscious design approach. The
designer must be aware of the quantities of nonrenewable resources used in the realization, operation,

and disposal of the built environment, and of the efficiency with which these resources are utilized. For instance, in a building design, the designer needs to be aware of the extent to which the spatial accommodation that he or she has designed exceeds or falls short of the building's requirements. Any difference in the provision of accommodation will represent the effectiveness with which energy and material resources are utilized by the designed system. Their quantification will represent the extent of the impact and use of the biosphere and the earth's resources by the designed system.

Simultaneously, in the totality of the biosphere, ecosystems and their processes also provide the final sink for all the discharges and wastes from the built environment. Since ecosystems have finite assimilative abilities, there is a similar limit to the extent to which discharges of waste products from the built environment can be permitted into ecosystems for assimilation. The designer now needs to be concerned with what will happen to the elements of the built environment at the end of their useful life, i.e., the extent of waste likely to be disposed of during use and the extent of waste likely to be deposited at the end of the built environment's physical life. We can conceive this in the form of a pattern of use or as a life cycle in order to trace the flow of resources through its economic and physical life. While the full quantification cannot be deterministically predicted, this process of evaluation ensures that the main undesirable impacts can be anticipated as far as possible.

3. *An ecosystem's contextual approach.* Not only do the components of the ecosystem interact with each

other within the ecosystem, ecosystems interact with other ecosystems and biospheric processes within the biosphere. The effects of human action on a specific ecosystem must not be seen by the designer as restricted to the confines of that ecosystem. The effects may synergistically extend to other ecosystems elsewhere.

In current architectural practice, a building site is usually delineated legally by its lot boundaries, whereas an ecosystem is delineated by its natural boundaries. Within an ecosystem there might be several building lots. The designer must not think of the project site as a discrete location that is isolated and defined exclusively and artificially by its legal boundaries. The ecological consequences of an action on a project site might extend to other lots within that ecosystem and to other ecosystems within the biosphere. The scale of such impacts might be determined by defining the areal impact of a design (i.e., local impacts, regional impacts, continental impacts, biosphere impacts).

4. *Project sites must be individually analyzed.* In the same way that no two biological specimens are exactly the same, each location is ecologically heterogeneous even though some may superficially appear to be similar. The designer must not view project sites as a uniform economic commodity with uniform ecosystem features. Each ecosystem has its own physical structure and composition of organisms, inorganic components, and interactions. During the site analysis stage, their individual values must be assessed by the designer, whether for preservation, conservation, or utilization. A specific design for one particular site

may not be repeatable for another site even though the spatial configuration of the sites may superficially appear similar (see Chap. 4).

5. *The life cycle design concept.* Interactions between ecosystems are dynamic processes and change over time. Ideally, we need to anticipate the impact and the performance of a designed system in the ecosystems throughout the entire span of the designed system's life cycle. At the same time, the states of the existing ecosystems are also changing. In architectural practice, the current restricted range of responsibilities of the designer would need to be expanded to include responsibilities for the environmental impacts of the designed system and its use over its physical life. Simultaneously, some form of environmental monitoring would be needed to check the impact of the designed system on its environment for the duration of its entire life span and also to monitor the changing state and response of the environment.

In the ecological approach, the designer must, in the preliminary design stages, predict insofar as possible the principal actions and activities associated with or resulting from the designed system during its anticipated life cycle. The designer must assess their possible impacts on the ecosystem and then anticipate these impacts in the design. The designer's responsibility needs to extend to a concern for the use of energy and materials by the designed system both before and after its construction (i.e., as a route flowing from resources' extraction from the environment to their eventual disposal as waste back into the environment).

6. *Building involves ecosystem spatial displacement and the addition of new energy and materials to the project site.* No matter how well designed, all built environments will spatially displace the ecosystem and add to the composition of the ecosystem of the project site by their physical presence. Their composition, siting, layout, land use, physical structure, and mechanical systems must be considered in relation to the ecosystem's components, spatial pattern, and functioning.

7. *The total-system or holistic approach.* The introduction of a designed system into an ecosystem may have multiple effects on the ecosystem. A simplistic or incremental design approach is unsatisfactory. Design must be seen in the context of the ecosystem operating as a whole and not in relation to any one of its components. The ecosystem approach is a holistic approach.

8. *The problem of the waste products disposal.* Generally, ecosystems have the ability to assimilate a certain amount of human intervention. However, there is a limit beyond which an ecosystem becomes irreparably damaged. An essential design goal should be to ensure that nothing in the existing order is permitted to become permanently lost or impaired as a result of human activities unless all foreseeable factors have been considered or the appropriate preventive action has been taken.

9. *Responsive and anticipatory design strategy.* The synthesis of any designed system will inevitably involve some environmental impact (whether in the form of an addition, alteration, or depletion) to the ecosystem, as well as some utilization and redistrib-

ution of the earth's resources. However, the fact that people alter ecosystems by their activities need not be held to be intrinsically undesirable or negative. Ecological design does not imply that the entire biosphere should be preserved entirely from human intervention, say, as a nature reserve. Neither is its goal to prevent all changes from taking place, since all ecosystems will change regardless of human action. The objective of ecological design is therefore not how to keep the biosphere and ecosystems from being influenced or changed by people, but of how to relate human activities to the ecosystems in the least destructive way, one that is within the inherent limitations of the ecosystem and most advantageous to the ecosystems. It should be possible in principle to design the built environment to have beneficial ecological impacts. The critical design issues are how, when, and where these changes are executed and what form of designed systems are introduced.

We can summarize the main assumptions that underlie our ecological approach to design as follows:

- It is advantageous for people to keep the environment biologically viable.
- The present state of progressive degradation of the environment by human actions is unacceptable.
- It is necessary to minimize people's destructive impacts on the ecosystems as far as possible.
- Natural resources are limited. Waste, once it is produced, is not easily regenerated.
- People are part of a closed system, and the processes of the natural environment, being unitary,

must be considered as part of the design and planning process.

- There are interrelationships between the man-made and the natural environment, and any changes to part of the system affect the entire system.

These premises are fundamental and vital to any ecological approach to design, and are essential factors that need to be considered in any design problem.

2

Architecture and Its Ecological Impact

Differences between the Designer's Traditional Concept of Architecture and the Ecologist's Concept of Architecture

Having examined the design implications of ecological concepts we need to examine the built environment and the role that it occupies in the biosphere from the point of view of the ecologist. The intention here is to look at the features of the built environment in order to identify those features which have ecological consequences or which influence the ecosystems, their structure and functioning, the earth's resources, and the biosphere as a whole.

In the same way that we have found that the designer's concept of the environment differs from the ecologist's concept, we now find a discrepancy between the ecologist's concept of the built environment and the designer's.

Traditionally, the designer sees building (architecture) in terms of its aesthetics, siting, spatial utilization, form, structure, building elements, use of color and shade, and other usual features of architectural design. However, the ecologist sees building in the context of the ecosystem concept. This means that he or she conceives a building as consisting of not only the abiotic (nonliving) components but also the biotic (living) components, all of which operate together as a whole system in the context of other ecosystems in the biosphere.

The ecologist also sees people as organisms, or biotic components in the ecosystems. As organisms, people consume food as energy and are part of the biosphere's food chain. Through their discharges of waste (human) and death, they provide decomposable matter to renew the nutrient pool in the biosphere (Williams and House, 1974). The difference is that although people are part of the biosphere's ecological cycle as terrestrial animals, they are also organisms that wield technological capacity outside of the ecological cycle. In this way, they are distinguishable from other organisms by the extent and magnitude of their abstracting and discharging activities (of the earth's energy and material resources) and by the complexity of their built environment and the subsystems by which the volume and pattern of abstraction and discharge are determined. Therefore, because of their extensive modification of the physical and biological milieus through their activities and built environment, people are now confronted by a number of environmental problems (Ehrenfield, 1970).

Although the biosphere's natural influences (e.g.,

earthquakes, erosion, geological crustal movement, fungal diseases, flora and fauna infestations) can also have catastrophic consequences on the ecosystems (Burton and Kates, 1964), our concern here is confined to environmental problems that are attributable to people and the built environment. As we have stated earlier, the environmental problems discussed here are the changes in ecosystem conditions and depletion of the earth's resources which arise from the stresses resulting from human action and activity (White, 1972). The changes in conditions caused by the built environment generally involve the depletion of, alteration of, and/or addition to the earth's ecosystems and resources. Any design action or activity which results in such changes may be regarded here as having an ecological impact.

The ecologist does not see the built environment separate from the ecosystems. Ecologically, people together with the built environment must be perceived to be part of the components and functioning of the ecosystems within the biosphere, even though we may find that their presence may cause conflicts with the ecosystems. Building construction is regarded by the ecologist as primarily a biotic activity.

We can conclude that in the ecological approach, the built environment must be analyzed using the ecosystem concept, that is, in terms of its structure of biotic and abiotic components, their interactions as a whole, and the flow of energy and materials through the system. However, as with most of the presently existing built environment, we find that it is largely the abiotic component (inorganic) that is predominant.

The Extent of Environmental Impact of a Built Environment Is Related to the Extent of Its User Requirements

Although it is characteristic of all life to take in suitable materials (e.g., food and air) and convert them into products of value to its own or its species' survival (e.g., heat), in contemporary human society the intake includes materials such as fossil fuels for energy (food and heat), shelter, and waste disposal (Detwyler and Marcus, 1972) (see Fig. 2-1 for an indication of the present level of consumption). It is therefore an inescapable fact that in order to provide people with these requirements for their existence, inevitable changes to the ecosystem will be incurred.

We can define our design task as the establishment of a "fit" between the pattern of needs and use: the patterns of built form, servicing systems, technological factors, and environmental factors (Martin, 1966). The design of any built environment is therefore determined by the extent of shelter and comfort required by the people who will use the designed system. This is often influenced by the socioeconomic-political structure of that society and its standard of living. It is these levels of needs and use that initially determine the size and extent of the pattern of built form and servicing systems.

It is therefore obvious that the environmental impact of humans increases when their demands for living conditions (i.e., their levels of needs and use) go beyond those of a "simple existence" (e.g., when they demand a steady food supply, heated and

Material	Minimum level of human consumption	Present level of consumption
1. Air	2.86×10 g oxygen/person/day (space capsule) (McHale, 1972)	Atmosphere is used extensively to assimilate pollutants
2. Water	2.5 L/person/day (primitive people) (Hamilton, 1971) 2.83 L/person/day (space capsule) (Konecci, 1964)	141 L/person/day (domestic) (U.K.) (Jeger, 1970) 132 L/person/day (trade) (U.K.) (Jeger, 1970) 273 L/person/day (national) (U.K.) (Jeger, 1970)
3. Shelter		20 m^2/person/dwelling (U.K.) (Morris, 1961) (equivalent to approx. 22×10 kWkt of building materials/person/dwelling) (Stelton, 1974)
4. Food	2×10 kcal/person/day (primitive people) (Cook, 1971) 0.68 kg/food/person/day (space capsule) (Konecci, 1964)	10×10 kcal/person/day (U.S.) (Cook, 1971)

Figure 2-1. The present level of human consumption.

Material	Minimum level of human consumption	Present level of consumption
5. Energy: mineral fuels		2.74 kW continuous average/person (U.K.) Petroleum: 413 L/person/annum (world average) (McHale, 1972) Natural gas: 161.3 m^3/person/annum (world average) (McHale, 1972) All mineral fuels: 8.06 $\times$ 10^3 kg/person annual production (U.S.) (Klaff, 1973)
6. Metals		Steel: 9400 kg in use/person (U.S.) (Brown, 1970) Copper: 150 kg in use/person (U.S.) (Brown, 1970) Lead: 150 kg in use/person (U.S.) (Brown, 1970) Al: 7100 kg in use/person (U.S.) (Brown, 1970) Zinc: 100 kg in use/person (U.S.) (Brown, 1970) Tin: 20 kg in use/person (U.S.) (Brown, 1970) All metals: 0.61 $\times$ 10^3 kg/person annual production (U.S.) (Klaff, 1973)

Figure 2-1. (*Continued*)

Material	Minimum level of human consumption	Present level of consumption
7. Nonmetallic minerals		Stone, sand, gravel: 3174 kg/person annual production (U.S.) (Ogburn, 1970) Cement: 226 kg/person annual production (U.S.) (Ogburn, 1970) Clay: 181 kg/person annual production (U.S.) (Ogburn, 1970) Common salt: 90 kg/person annual production (U.S.) (Ogburn, 1970) Phosphate rock: 45/kg person annual production (U.S.) (Ogburn, 1970) All nonmetallic minerals: 9.31×10^3 kg/person annual production (U.S.) (Ogburn, 1970)

Figure 2-1. (*Continued*)

cooled shelters, mobility). The more people depart from a simple pattern of existence, the more complex is the support that they will draw from the environment, and consequently the more they have to plan for and expect environmental impairment. For instance, a reduction in human environmental influence is possible, but only at the expense of a reduction in the provision for shelter and comfort.

Material	Minimum level of human consumption	Present level of consumption
8. Organic materials (nonfood)		1.27×10^3 kg/person annual production (U.S.) (Klaff, 1973)
9. Waste disposal:		
Gases	2.4 kg/person/day (space capsule) (Konecci, 1964)	0.86 kg air pollutants/person/day (U.S.) (Wolman, 1965)
Liquid	1.9 kg/person/day (space capsule) (Konecci, 1964)	
Solid	0.1 kg/person/day (space capsule) (Konecci, 1964)	32 kg/person/day (household, commercial, and municipal) (U.S.) (USDH, 1968) 1.4 kg/person/day (industrial) (U.S.) (USDH, 1968) 6.8 kg/person/day (agricultural) (U.S.) (USDH, 1968) 19.1 kg/person/day (animal) (U.S.) (USDH, 1968) 14.0 kg/person/day (mineral) (U.S.) (USDH, 1968)

Figure 2-1. (*Continued*)

The less that is demanded by people from the ecosystems, therefore, the less will be their impact on them. If people had no need for shelter and comfort, then there would be no necessity for an ecological approach to the design of the built environment.

We can conclude that in the ecological approach, the designer must design with the premise that the human impact increases in relation to the increase in demands for living conditions beyond those of a simple existence. In the design process, before the designer proceeds with the design, he or she must first review the design brief and find out the extent of shelter and comfort that he or she must design for. The following decisions have to be made:

- What is the present standard of living conditions?
- What is the proposed standard of living conditions that the users require?
- What are they willing to give up or tolerate to have it?

If the designer were to attempt to keep the adverse environmental impacts of a design to an absolute minimum, then it would mean that society would have to return to a much simpler form of existence, to living conditions that make fewer demands for environmental comfort, shelter, energy, and materials consumption than the present conditions do. However, this would require a complex and extensive restructuring of the existing sociological, economic, and political structures, which is obviously outside the realm of the designer. In many design programs, it is unfortunate that the design brief has already been largely determined by others and by the society that the designer is operating within. A designer might be said to be a problem solver who is free to decide which problems should be solved. However, in most cases, the problems and often the solutions are set for the designer by others. The requirements and the environmental design conditions as well as the financial budget are often determined even before the designer has been approached.

Given the existing socioeconomic-political limitations of the society in which the designer operates, he or she can either attempt to change the existing order and its limitations or design with the strategy of "buying time," to allow society to make the necessary adjustments to a more ecologically responsive social and consumption habit, living pattern, and values, and to enable the development of the appropriate environmentally responsive technologies.

In the latter approach, the designer's strategy would be to try to keep the anticipated destructive impacts of the designed system to a minimum and to maintain the overall stability of the ecosystems, insofar as possible. In this case, our designed system can be said to represent a statement by the designer of the extent of the impact of the designed system on the environment which has been accepted and anticipated by the designer and by the people who use it. In this way, design anticipates the role of the impacts that the designed system will have on the environment. Prediction of the ecological impacts of a proposed design must therefore become an essential factor in all design decisions.

The Built Environment as an Open System and as Part of the Flow of Energy and Materials within the Biosphere

The total ecological effect of any built environment that is constructed is the increase in the human presence in the ecosystems, i.e., the addition to the already extensive modification of the ecosystems. The urban and industrial built environment, in particular, are humanity's most intensively serviced and managed systems. They consume substantial portions of the earth's resources (including space) for their realization and operation, and they also contribute a substantial portion of the by-products in the biosphere. Like a living organism, the present built environment's life-support systems require constant inputs and make constant outputs. Viewing the built environment in this way has certain advantages. Since the extraction and processing of all material and energy resources for the built environment involve changes to the ecosystems (as well as some depletion of the earth's finite nonrenewable resources), the designer needs to be aware of the extent of the earth's material and energy resources used as inputs in the composition of any designed system because the specific use of each material and energy resource in the built environment incurs spatial alterations to the ecosystems as well as a depletion of that resource.

With the ecosystem concept, we can analytically break down the physical elements of a building into those biotic and abiotic elements of the earth which have been part-by-part processed or assembled by people into the built environment. The design of the built environment can be conceived as a form of management of energy and material resources. In this way, every element of a designed system can be accounted for and traced to its source. Instead of conceiving the built environment traditionally as a static and immutable object, it should more appropriately be viewed as part of the continuous flow and exchange of energy and materials within the biosphere (in the same way that an ecologist might view the flow of energy and materials through an ecosystem) (e.g., Odum, E. P., 1963).

In the ecological approach, any building in the ecosystem represents only a transient phase, in which people have assembled a quantity of energy and matter into certain predetermined patterns and forms of use on that ecosystem. Then at the end of the useful life of the building, the materials are often removed and disposed of elsewhere or reused. Thus, if we are to view the situation holistically, then we can contend that every designed system and every element of that system represent only one minute segment in the biosphere's continuous exchanges and cycles of energy and materials (see Fig. 2-2). By conceiving the built environment in this way, the designer is forced to view the man-made environment synoptically as part of the biosphere and as a subordinate system which is dependent on the biosphere for its existence. He or she is directed to account for the quantities of material and energy that flow through the designed system and through the man-made environment (see Fig. 2-3) and to account for the environmental disturbances that result. This dependency is the crux upon which our ecological approach to design is based. If we view the man-made environment in this way, we need to trace the routes by which the earth's material and energy resources are transferred from their source into the man-made environment and finally reintroduced into the environment. Usually, it is at the *transfer points* that inefficient technological performance and bad design may lead to excessive ecosystem impairment. This can occur at the point of

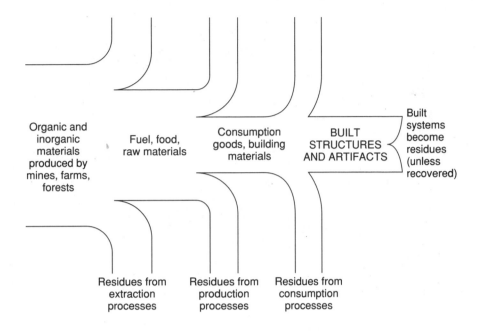

| Organic and inorganic materials produced by mines, farms, forests | Fuel, food, raw materials | Consumption goods, building materials | BUILT STRUCTURES AND ARTIFACTS | Built systems become residues (unless recovered) |

| Residues from extraction processes | Residues from production processes | Residues from consumption processes |

Residues: solids, particulates, gases, heat, liquids, etc.

Figure 2-2. The built environment as part of the flow of energy and materials.

extraction of raw materials from the earth (e.g., transportation, construction, operation, recovery) or at the point of discharge of these energy and material resources by the built environment. The extent will depend on the particular type of energy resource or material resource. For example, aluminum has a higher energy cost of production and environmental pollution than iron.

In the ecological approach to design, the designer must therefore be concerned not only with the extent and range of human use of the ecosystem and the earth's resources in the designed system, but also with the way in which these elements are abstracted, stored, assembled, used, and finally dis-

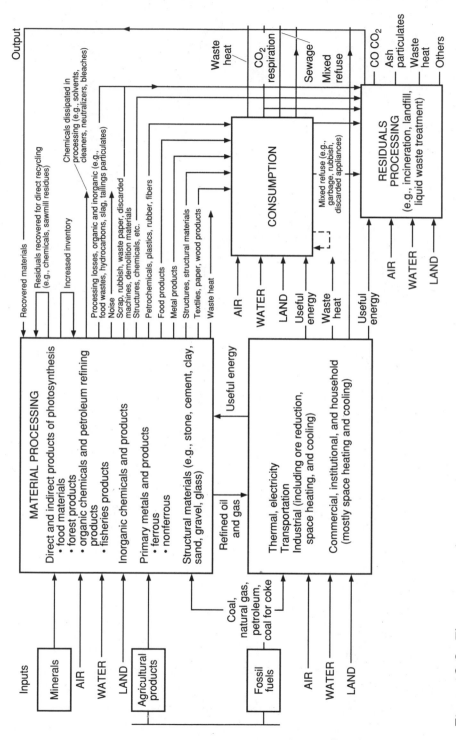

Figure 2-3. The inputs and outputs through the built environment (adapted from Kneese et al., 1971, and elaborated).

posed of (or reintroduced) into the biosphere.

We can conclude that in order to fully appreciate the ecological implications of any design, the designer will need to analyze the built environment in terms of its flow of energy and materials throughout its life cycle from their source of origin to their sink. Following from this analysis, the designer must simultaneously anticipate at the design stage all the desirable impacts on the ecosystems along this route. This analysis can be conveniently conceived using the concept of an *open system*, i.e., in terms of inputs into the system, functions within the system, outputs from the system, and the relationship of the environment to the system.

The Activities Associated with a Designed System and the Operational Functions within the Designed System

As we have discussed earlier, the built environment is an artificial man-made component of the ecosystem which has been designed to provide certain predetermined functions and services for people (whether physical, spatial, social, cultural, etc.). Generally, it can be described as the designed environment that is constructed by people to bring them protection from the natural elements, provide comfort, house their assisting devices (e.g., equipment and machinery), and increase their effectiveness and that of their devices. The built environment is designed to enable a range of activities and operations to take place within its physical framework.

The built environment therefore consists of not only its physical structure but also the human actions and activities in the designed system and the operational functions of the designed system's mechanical subsystems and biotic components. We can term these the internal relations of the built environment.

In the normal process of design, the designer has to determine and predict those functions and operational activities that will take place within the designed system. In the ecological approach, the designer has the additional task of assessing the anticipated impact of each of these actions and activities on the ecosystem. In the process of doing this, the features of the ecosystem of that location and their resilience to changes will provide the environmental criteria to determine whether the range of actions and activities associated with the designed system and the operational functions of the designed life-support system may be permitted on that ecosystem. (See Chap. 4.)

The Biological Structure of the Built Environment

In most existing urban and industrial environments, there usually remains very little of the natural shape and structure of the original locality's ecosystem after urban or industrial development has taken place. The previous biological structure and functional complexity of the ecosystems on which the building development took place are often replaced by a simpler, more synthetic, and increasingly homogenized abiotic type of environment (e.g., concrete, asphalt, paving). Particularly, with the creation of permanent urban settlements (e.g., towns and cities) the built environment has become more and more synthetic and intentionally remote in its interaction with the ecosystems in the biosphere.

The fact that people are constantly moving into new environments (e.g., through aerospace travel) tends to give the impression that they are enlarging the range of their evolutionary past (Dubos, 1967). This is an illusion because wherever people go, they can function only to the extent that they maintain a microenvironment that is similar to the one from which they evolved, i.e., the ecosystems. This has been demonstrated in the design of micro-life-support systems for use in extreme environments, such as aquatic and extraterrestrial exploration expeditions (Odum, H. T., 1963; Konecci and Wood, 1969; etc.). In the design of these micro-life-support systems, it has been found that people must be linked to the earth by an umbilical cord, or alternatively must be confined in enclosures which almost duplicate certain essential processes of terrestrial ecosystems. In some examples of the latter type of micro-support systems, a certain amount of the inputs necessary for the survival of the system can be stored. For a longer survival time, a more biological structure, similar to that of a terrestrial ecosystem, would be needed.

Such a life-support system must include not only the vital biotic substances and the means to recycle them but also the vital biotic components. Processes like production, consumption, and decomposition must be performed in a balanced manner by the biotic components or else by some mechanical substitutes which have to be designed into the life-support system (Cooke et al., 1968). If its long-term survival is to be ensured, then the "life-support system" of a designed system must include all three of the basic biotic components found in the structure of the earth's ecosystem (producers, consumers, decomposers) in similar biological proportion and diversity (Odum, E. P., 1971). The analogy is clear. The built environment should ideally possess a full complement of an ecosystem's components and processes. For instance, the locally diverse ecological assemblages of terrestrial ecosystems harbor certain controlling species whose interspecies relations check the growth of many potential pest species. When the natural diversity of the ecosystem's components is reduced (as by human interference) and the controlling species eliminated, the problems of pest control in the ecosystem increase (Institute of Ecology, 1972). Otherwise, the alternative of reducing the number of species in an ecosystem to, say, two species (e.g., humans and a plant species) would require the substitution of extensive engineering systems to replace the existent biological circuitry. This is undesirable, since it is difficult to duplicate the full range of components of a terrestrial ecosystem and still ensure the long-term autonomous survival of the designed system. Ideally, design should aim at a compatible combination of components.

If we examine our existing urban areas as man-made ecosystems, we find that they possess an incomplete biological structure. They contain no significant numbers of green plants carrying on photosynthesis to produce food and fibers for human consumption. The existing built environment is totally dependent on its surrounding regions and agricultural ecosystems to supply it with food and other resources and to handle its residues and discharges. It is generally devoid of any mutually beneficial relationship with the ecosystems.

This analogy of the biological structure of the existing built environment with that of an ecosystem is clear. In many respects, the problems of survival in an isolated man-made micro-life-support system (as in a spacecraft) resemble the problems encountered in humans' continued survival in the "global life-support system" or the biosphere (Fuller, 1963; Linton et al., 1967; Boulding, 1969; McHarg, 1969b; McHale, 1972; etc.). We find, for instance, that the detection and control of air pollution and water contamination, the adequate supply and nutritional quality of food, and the management of the accumulated toxic wastes and residues are common environmental problems of both micro-life-support systems designed for extreme environments and built systems in the biosphere.

If we are to ensure the built environment's long-term survival in the biosphere, then its systems must have certain obligatory relationships with the ecosystems and their processes. Rather than being designed to be totally isolated from the ecosystems, the built environment should be designed to integrate and have compatible symbiotic relationships with the ecosystems. In occupying any location, a designed system has at the same time assumed an ecological role (whether contributory or passive) in relation to that ecosystem's composition and function. In the ecological approach, this role is part of the designer's responsibility. The designer must ensure that the designed system exists and responds

as an integral component of the ecosystems, not as
an isolated system severed from any relationship
with the project site's ecosystem, nor as a system
which is completely dependent (parasitic) on the
surrounding ecosystems.

Structuring the Relationship between a Designed System and Its Environment

The built environment is analogous to a living system (or organism), which survives by importing
energy and matter from its environment in one form
or another and then exporting it back into its environment after use (i.e., exchanges of energy and
materials). In the ecological approach, we may view
our built environment and its operation as being
principally concerned with the organization, distribution, use, and management of energy and matter.

This implies that our traditional concept of architecture has to be modified so that it is seen as a form
of management of energy and materials or as an
organization of the flow of energy and matter
between the designed system and its environment.
Our designed system can be seen as a system that is
connected to the ecosystems within the biosphere by
the various subsystems and flow of inputs and outputs in which energy and matter are converted by
the metabolism of the system. We can describe this
relationship simply with a familiar input-output
structural model (Fig. 2-4).

However, as we have pointed out earlier, our
designed system can also be viewed in two other

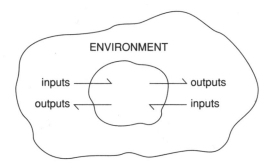

Figure 2-4. A simple model of a system and its environment and the exchanges between the two.

ways. It can be seen as an entity consisting of the operational activity that takes place within the system (i.e., its internal relations) and it can be seen also as an entity consisting of the system's physical composition and form (or its elements). Bringing these together, the structure of our system now represents the collection of the elements and relations belonging to that system (Saragasti, 1970).

However, we must also include in our model the external environment with which it has interactions. We can now further elaborate on the previous simple model of inputs and outputs, developing a model which includes the system's elements, its internal relations, and its external relations with its environment (Fig. 2-5).

This basic structural model of the relationship between a designed system and its environment can be further expanded by setting out the boundaries so that the fluxes across the boundaries are functional specifications and the processes within the boundaries are system functions (Peranio, 1973).

For instance, with a further elaborated model (Fig. 2-6), we can conceive the built environment as being

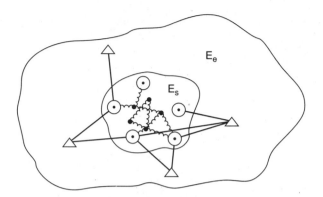

where E_e = environment of the system under investigation

E_s = the system under investigation

△ = elements members of E_e

☉ = boundary members of E_s

• = internal elements of E_s

— = external relations

〜〜〜 = internal relations

⌒ = boundary defining the elements

Figure 2-5. Systems and elements. This model can be used to describe a living system (e.g., an ecosystem) as well as the built environment.

analogous to the ecosystem and to consist of the following attributes:

- The system's abiotic components, with its content of energy matter and information inside its boundaries (the built system and the physical elements).
- The system's biotic components (fauna, flora, people).
- The environment with which the system exchanges energy/matter inputs and outputs (the ecological environment).
- A source of energy/matter which flows through the boundary and into the system (the inputs).

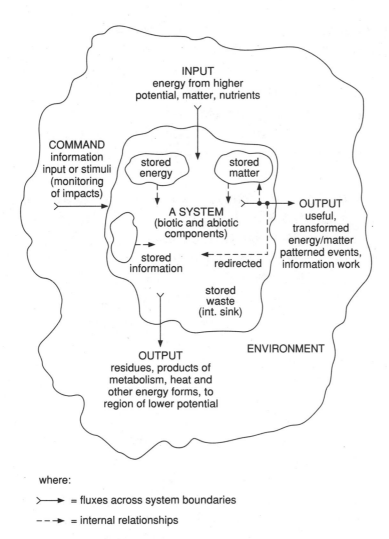

Figure 2-6. An input-output structural model of the built environment.

- A source of information constituting the patterned events coming from the environment outside the boundaries of the system, and/or derived from within the boundaries of the system itself (the monitoring system).

- The processes of the system and its components in which the energy/matter inputs are either directly used or kept within the boundaries of the system for use at another time (the system metabolism).
- The flow through the boundary of the system of energy and/or matter which constitutes the rejects of the system as a consequence of the system's processes (reject outputs).
- The flow out of the system to other systems and to the environment, which takes the form of matter and/or energy that becomes available to produce physical effects or useful products. These can be either directed out of the system, used directly, and/or kept for future use (useful outputs).
- The processes of the system environment which are affected by the functioning of the system, and which affect the system (ecosystem processes).
- The interactions of the above (state of the system).

Based on the open-system concept, we can now provide and structure a model of our designed system of varying complexity, depending on its use in the design process, in a way that is analogous to the ecosystem, i.e., from the point of view of the ecologist. Each of these interactions is interrelated with the others as well as with the earth's ecosystems and resources.

From examining the built environment from the ecologist's point of view, we can now summarize those features and aspects of our built environment that have ecological implications and affect our design implications. These are as follows:

1. *The built environment possesses abiotic and biotic components.* The architect tends to see architecture in

terms of its aesthetics, siting, spatial utilization, form, structure, and building elements, whereas the ecologist regards the built environment as a product of a biotic activity—people are simply one of the biotic components in the biosphere. The built environment becomes regarded as consisting of both biotic (organic) and abiotic (inorganic) components assembled by people to provide themselves with certain functions.

2. *Design involves setting the standards of living and minimizing user requirements.* The impact of a design is related to the size and context of the designed requirements. Design involves the setting down of standards for the built environment. The extent of accommodation provided by the designer depends on the level of needs of the people who will use the built environment. The higher the level of needs, the more extensive will be the size of the built environment, and therefore the greater its ecological impact. If one accepts the fact that building (architecture) is now a prerequisite for human existence, then the question would be: In what way could architecture be designed, built, and utilized to have minimum impact on the earth's ecosystems? A reduction in environmental impacts can be effected if there is a similar reduction in the demands by people for their needs, e.g., shelter, comfort, mobility, and food supply. We conclude that, ultimately, the extent of the impact of any design is related to the society that commissioned it. The designer must initially examine the design brief and make decisions as to what has to be provided and what is not to be provided in the design. The less that needs to be provided, the less will be the ecological impact.

3. *The built environment considered as part of the flow of energy and materials in its life cycle.* In the ecological approach to design, the designer must be concerned not only with the extent and the range of people's needs and use of the biosphere's ecosystems and the earth's resources (as inputs), but also with the way in which these elements are abstracted, stored, assembled, used, and finally disposed of (or reintroduced) into the biosphere (as outputs). To facilitate this task, the designer can see the built environment conceptually as a flow of energy and materials (from their source of origin in the earth to their sink) over a life cycle. In this way, at the design stage we can conceive the built environment as a form of management of energy and materials. In analyzing this flow, we can simultaneously anticipate its impacts on the ecosystems, with the goal of minimizing all undesirable impacts.

4. *The need to integrate the designed system with the earth's ecosystems.* It is not necessary to design the built environment to exactly duplicate or imitate the biological structure and processes in the ecosystem because it is not necessary to design systems which exist in total isolation from the environment. The design goal is to restrict the undesirable ecosystem impacts and interactions of the designed system so that they are as localized geographically as possible, to conserve resources, and to integrate or seek compatible and mutually beneficial relationships between the designed system and the ecosystem (e.g., Brown, 1985; Pearson, 1989).

5. *Identification of the impacts incurred in the life cycle of a designed system.* In the ecological approach to design, the built environment can be conceived in

two ways. A designed system can be seen first as an entity consisting of biotic and abiotic components (its elements) and second as an entity consisting of the operational activities which take place within the system or associated with it. Furthermore, the system's physical substance (its elements) does not exist as a static component of the environment, but interacts as part of the overall flow of materials and energy through the biosphere over time. In this way, we see the designed system holistically as part of the earth and its processes. As mentioned earlier, a designed system requires inputs from the environment for its realization, operation, and disposal; and it emits outputs. In the process, the total environmental impact of a designed system is the net result of not only the impacts from the system's own operational activity but also the impacts caused by all the activities involved in the construction of the built system's physical substance and form and the impacts that the use of these elements, their disposal, and their recovery for reuse will generate. It is necessary to identify the impacts incurred in the entire life cycle of the designed system.

6. *The external context of a designed system consists of the totality of the ecosystems in the biosphere and the earth's resources.* The external dependencies of a designed system (i.e., its environmental dependencies) consist of the totality of the ecosystems in the biosphere and the earth's resources. For instance, a designed system spatially displaces the ecosystems by its spatial presence and depletes the earth's energy and material resources by its creation, operation, and disposal. The utilization of the earth's resources for the designed system further involves extensive

modifications to the ecosystems when the resources are extracted or made available.

To summarize, we can conceive of a designed system's impacts on the ecosystems and its external environment conveniently by considering the interactions that take place between, first, its exchanges of inputs and outputs, second, the operational activities within the designed system, and, third, its external environment, which consists of the earth's ecosystems and resources (see Chap. 4 for our interactions framework). With any designed system, a thorough understanding of these impacts is the crux of our ecological approach to design. We can conclude here that all architecture (or building) will have the following forms of impact upon the earth's ecological systems and resources:

- It spatially displaces a portion of the ecosystem by its physical presence. Simultaneously, its composition of energy and materials modifies that ecosystem's composition of energy and materials.

- After its construction, the use of a built environment encourages other human activities and other building developments to take place, which will incur further recurring environmental impacts. A designed system affects and is affected by its environment during its useful life.

- It depletes the earth's nonrenewable resources by consuming vast quantities of energy and material resources for its realization, operation, and disposal. In addition to the depletion of resources, the process of extracting and making these resources available for use in the built environment uses up more energy and material resources and also inflicts considerable impact on the ecosystems.

- It emits large quantities of outputs, including discharges of waste energy (heat) and materials (e.g., pollutants) as a result of its realization, operation, and disposal. These outputs can affect the functioning of the earth's ecosystems, the functioning of other built environments, and the earth's future supply of resources.

We can conclude that the ecologist conceives the built environment as an entity consisting of not only the built system's physical substance and form, but of the operational activity that takes place within it. It is essential that we identify the environmental impacts of that designed system, including not only those inherent in the making and building of the elements, but also those that the use of these elements, their disposal, and their recovery will generate. By looking at any designed system from the point of view of these interactions we are in a position to anticipate holistically those aspects of the designed system that have ecological impacts as part of our design process.

3
Framework for Ecological Design

The Need for a Structure for Design

Ecological architecture is a designed system that seeks to minimize and at the same time is responsive to the negative impacts that it has on the earth's ecosystems and resources. Therefore, the framework for design should be one that structures its interactions with the earth's ecosystems and resources in such a way that we can identify those that are undesirable and need to be minimized or altered through design synthesis.

Generally, in the analysis of any designed system and its environment, there is essentially no limit to the number of variables that we can include in the analysis or in description of the situation. No matter how fortunate our choice of inputs and outputs to enter into the description of that system and its environment may be, they cannot be expected to constitute a complete description. The crucial task in any theory building is to pick the right variables to be included.

73

It is therefore useful for the designer to possess a set of organizing principles in the form of an open structure with which the selected and relevant design constraints (e.g., ecological considerations) can be organized. Furthermore, the structure needs to enable the organization of the design constraints in relation to each other to facilitate their selection, consideration, and incorporation in design synthesis. This open structure can be in the form of a conceptual or theoretical framework. The open structure must be general in nature in order to allow the designer to decide which ecological considerations to incorporate in the design synthesis. Using an open structure, the designer can also include any other related and pertinent disciplines that are similarly concerned with the problems of environmental protection and conservation.

The Design Process as a Form of Preparation of an Environmental Impact Statement

From the earlier examination of ecology and ecological concepts, we have determined that the extent of the environmental consequences of any built system can be seen in relation to the extent of its demands and dependencies on the earth's ecosystems and processes and on the earth's energy and material resources (e.g., for a specific product or a specific service). If the designer is aware of the ecological consequences of the design, then the designed system represents in effect a summation of the extent of its impacts on the environment that has been accepted and anticipated by the designer. Our design task might be better viewed in this light as a form of preparation of an environmental impact statement. Defining the design task in this way does not mean an exploitative role of people in the biosphere (Bookchin, 1973). On the contrary, this approach emphasizes the extent of people's dependency and that of their built structures on the biosphere and on the earth's resources. Such a viewpoint would focus our attention on the identification of those aspects of the designed system which have ecological implications and indicate the critical areas where the undesirable impacts might be eliminated, reduced, or remedied. In the ecological approach, the realization of any designed system is therefore seen to be dependent directly or indirectly upon the biosphere for specific elements and processes, which can be identified generally as:

- A supplier of certain products, resources, or goods (renewable and nonrenewable), e.g., minerals, fossil fuels, air, water, and food
- A supplier of certain processes (biological, physical, and chemical), e.g., for biological decomposition, photosynthesis, mineral cycling, and gaseous exchange
- A receiver of the residues and discharges resulting from the metabolism, activities, and processes of humans and their man-made systems, e.g., land disposal of wastes
- A spatial environment in which human actions and activities take place, e.g., recreation, construction, and access

It should be pointed out that these aspects over-

lap to some extent and that they have been identified in this way in order to emphasize the transfer
points or the points of exchange. It is usually at
these points of exchange that poorly designed interactions result in environmental impairment. For
instance, the linkages and transfer points between
these dependencies can be traced schematically in
Fig. 3-1. We should take care to note that the concept
of a designed system that is absolutely ecologically
compatible is impractical because it is an inescapable fact that any built structure's synthesis will

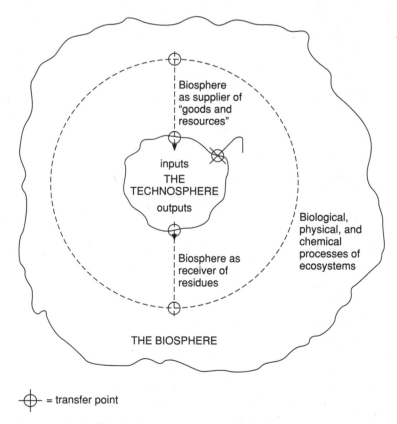

⊕ = transfer point

Figure 3-1. The linkages between the built environment and its external environment.

involve some loss to the biosphere, whether to a greater or lesser extent. It is not possible to design a system in which these linkages have no impacts on the ecosystem. The most that can be expected of built structures is that they have low or minimum destructive impacts on the environment.

The synthesis of any built structure therefore represents a net statement of its demands and its influences on the ecosystems and the earth's resources. To determine these demands and influences, we must trace the uses of energy and materials in the designed system in the form of routes flowing from their environmental sources to the system's dependencies. With this concept, all the attributes of a designed system (whether functional, spatial, economic, cultural, etc.) would have to be seen in the context of their relationship to the ecological environment. Only by identifying the dependencies associated with each design can the undesirable impacts on the ecosystems be assessed and minimized, and preventive action taken. Any such framework for design would ideally structure these dependencies into a whole to show their interrelationships.

A Framework for Identifying the Ecological Criteria in the Design and Planning of the Built Environment

In our synthesis of a framework, the following factors need to be considered:

- A framework for ecological design should include the following components: the designed system (our system under study or to be designed), the environment of the designed system (which includes the earth's ecosystems and resources), and any interactions between the designed system and its environment.

- Any designed system has both a physical composition and form and its own set of operational functions, all of which interact with its environment spatially and systemically over time.

- Like a living system, the designed system requires continuous inputs of energy and materials, and makes outputs of energy and materials into its environment. A model which can structure the interactions between a designed system and the ecological environment in terms of these exchanges would therefore be advantageous because such a model would force us, first, to determine the internal activity that takes place within the system, and second, to measure the designed system's dependence upon the ecological environment in terms of the energy and matter that are taken from it and returned to it as a result of the internal activity.

- We need also to examine the built environment within the spatial context of the ecosystems in which its activities take place, so that we can identify the accompanying consequences of these activities on the ecosystems.

We can now structure those relationships between ecosystems and the built environment explicitly in a framework of sets of interactions (vis-à-vis impacts) between the built environment and the ecological environment. These interactions are analogous to the concept of an open system. Based on the above features, interactions can be classified into four general sets:

1. The external interdependencies of the designed system (its external or environmental relations)
2. The internal interdependencies of the designed system (its internal relations)
3. The external-to-internal exchanges of energy and matter (its inputs)
4. The internal-to-external exchanges of energy and matter (its outputs)

We should note that these four sets of interactions correspond to our earlier description of the transfer points and dependencies that architecture makes on the earth's ecosystems and resources. In any ecological approach to design, we must simultaneously consider all four of these aspects as well as their interrelationships with each other.

To demonstrate the interrelationships of these sets of interactions, we can further structure them into a symbolic form as follows: Given a designed system and its environment, let suffix 1 denote the system under consideration and suffix 2, the environment around that system. Further, let letter L be the interdependent connections within the framework. It follows that four types of interactions can be identified in the analysis (Tolman and Brunswick, 1935; Emery and Trist, 1965; Walmsley, 1972): $L11$, $L12$, $L21$, and $L22$. This can be further represented in the form of a partitioned matrix (LP) as follows:

$$(LP) = \begin{array}{c|c} L11 & L12 \\ \hline L21 & L22 \end{array}$$

where

$L11$ refers to the processes and activities that take place within the system or the area of internal interdependencies

$L22$ refers to the processes and activities that take place in the environment of the system, or the external interdependencies

$L12$ refers to the exchanges of the system with its environment, or the transactional interdependencies of the system/environment

$L21$ refers to the exchanges of the environment with the system, or the transactional interdependencies of the environment/system

The above model constitutes our interactions framework. It provides the designer with a unifying concept, which he or she can apply as a holistic, inclusive, and open structure for the ecological interactions (organized in the form of sets of environmental interdependencies) of the designed system. By using this as a structural tool, the designer can examine any designed system and determine its inputs, outputs, and internal and external relations, then ascertain which of their ecological impacts need to be given priority and which need to be taken into account or adjusted in the process of design improvement and development. In this way, any designed system can be conceptually broken down and analyzed using these four sets of interactions. For instance, we can interpret the components of the interactions framework as shown in Fig. 3-2.

Interactions	Symbol	Description
The external interdependencies of the designed system (its external relations)	L22	This refers to the totality of the ecological processes of the surrounding ecosystems which interact with other ecosystems elsewhere within the biosphere, and the totality of the earth's resources. It also includes the slow biospheric processes involved in the formation of fossil fuels and other nonrenewable resources. These may influence the built environment's functioning and are in turn also influenced by the built environment. It is these elements which are either altered, depleted, or added to by the built environment.
The internal interdependencies of the designed system (its internal relations	L11	This refers to the sum of the activities and actions that take place in or are related to and associated with the built environment and its users. They include the operational functions of the built environment. These will directly affect the ecosystems of the location in which they take place spatially and the ecosystems elsewhere (systemically) as well as the earth's totality of resources. These can be considered in the pattern of a life cycle of the built environment.

Figure 3-2. Description of interactions.

Interactions	Symbol	Description
The external/ internal exchanges of energy and matter (the system's inputs)	$L21$	This refers to the total inputs into the built environment. These consist of both the stock and the flow components of the built environment (or the energy and matter needed for the physical substance and form of the built environment and for the operations of the built environment and its attendant processes). The efforts taken to process these inputs from the earth's resources often result in considerable disruption and undesirable consequences to the ecosystems.
The internal/ external exchanges of energy and matter (the system's outputs)	$L12$	This refers to the total outputs of energy and matter that are discharged from the built environment into the ecosystems and into the earth. These outputs may include the built environment's own physical substance and form, which also may need to be disposed of at the end of its useful life. These outputs, if they are not assimilated by the ecosystems, result in environmental impairment.

Figure 3-2. (*Continued*)

Design Implications

Ecological design is an anticipatory approach to design. It must be one that is critical of its influences over the earth's ecosystems and resources and one that is responsive to their inherent constraints and opportunities. In the design process, the designer must comprehensively take into account the antici-pated adverse effects that the product of that design process will have on the earth's ecosystems and resources, and simultaneously give priority to the elimination and minimization of these adverse effects.

From the ecological point of view, we have earlier redefined and reconceived our process of architec-tural design to be concerned with energy and mate-rials management. The earth's energy and material resources (biotic and abiotic components) are man-aged and assembled by the designer into a tempo-rary form (viz., for the period of intended use), then demolished at the end of this period and either recy-cled within the built environment or assimilated into the natural environment.

The ecologist conceives the built environment as an entity consisting of not only the built system's physical substance and form, but also the opera-tional activity that takes place within it. In the design process, it is essential that we identify the environmental interactions of that designed system, including not only those inherent in the making and building of the elements, but also the impacts that the use of these elements, their disposal, and their recovery will generate.

The interactions framework is useful as a design tool because it enables the designer to simultaneously structure and relate the ecological aspects of the built environment into a unified set of interrelated interactions. The designer can now use this framework to decompose and analyze any proposed design and its elements into the following components: the designed system's exchanges of energy and materials (its inputs and outputs), its internal relations, and its external relations with the ecosystems and the earth's resources. The designer's responsibility would then be to chart and to anticipate all the aspects of the designed system which could have undesirable environment impacts, while at the same time keeping in mind the overall ecological design objectives of keeping the environment biologically viable, limiting the degradation of the environment by human activities, and minimizing people's destructive impacts on the ecosystems as far as possible.

As we have described earlier, in this form of structural analysis, the framework forces the designer to view the total set of environmental impacts (interactions) of the designed system and their interrelationships simultaneously, and to determine which considerations need to be incorporated in the designed system. The framework also serves as an environmental impact matrix for a designed system. In this way, it simply provides a design approach based on the designer's resolution of these anticipated impacts and interactions into a suitable built form. Since the interactions are interdependent, if the designer by mistake omits any, this could result in an imbalance somewhere in the ecosystems. For instance, a design which places particular emphasis on the reduction of emissions from the designed systems (i.e., the pollutive outputs) might eventually require an excessive consumption of energy resources (inputs) in order to maintain the system. The designer is reminded by the framework that any design approach which does not comprehensively consider the full set of interactions will ultimately be unsatisfactory in its relationship with the ecosystems. In the process of selecting the designed system's physical fabric and technical subsystems, the designer's objectives must be to integrate the designed system's components systemically and spatially with the project site's ecosystems and to seek symbiotic and compatible relationships with the environment (see Chap. 8 for implications on design decisions). However, we should note that the framework simply provides a theoretical structure for design action and does not include the feedback of the system that is being designed. For instance, the outputs emitted from a designed system into its environment may influence the environment's potential to supply inputs to the designed system (Miller, 1966). To include such feedback, a more elaborate and dynamic model must be derived from this model.

The comprehensiveness of the model is one of its important features. Previously, the term *ecological design* has been loosely used by many designers (e.g., Wells, 1972) to refer to any approach to design that expresses some concern for its impact on the environment.

However, since the ecosystem approach is a comprehensive and synoptic approach, any other approach which does not take into account the entire set of interdependencies in our interactions framework cannot be considered an ecological design. Any piecemeal or incomplete approach to environmental problems may result in creating further environment problems to add to the ones that were originally intended to be redressed.

The interactions framework has four prime functions:

1. It provides the designer with a conceptual and structural tool for simultaneously analyzing and examining the ecological consequences of the built environment. After they have been identified in this process, those interactions would need to be further synthesized into a physical form by the designer through selection of the appropriate technological subsystems and materials (see Chap. 8 for a discussion on design decisions).

2. The framework provides a common frame of reference that the designer and others from related disciplines can use to look at any particular environmental problem (e.g., pollution), thus ensuring a comprehensive examination of its interrelationship with other environmental problems. With this framework, future theoretical development is facilitated, since the structure can also serve as a basis for unifying other related work in this area of study. Other approaches that share similar concerns for environmental problems and previously have been carried out independently can now be assessed and unified by this structure (e.g., resource conservation can be considered part of the input analysis to a built environment). Those disciplines concerned with environmental protection and conservation can now be brought together into

a coherent philosophy for ecological design. Our interactions framework provides us with a single unifying theory that encompasses all those aspects of environmental protection and conservation which have previously been unrelated.

3. The framework has a wider use in that it provides a structure for assessing the environmental implications of other human actions or activities besides the creation of a built environment, e.g., recreational activities, tourism, etc.

4. The framework serves to point out and span the void in present design theory and research. For instance, the interactions framework would indicate the type of data necessary to quantify its own components and would further provide a quantitative tool that the designer could use in evaluating a proposed design and comparing it with another.

We will examine and explore each of the four components of the framework in greater detail in the next four chapters.

4

External Ecological Interdependencies of the Built Environment

The Dependencies of the Built Environment as a Spatial Environment

The external ecological interdependencies of the built environment consist of the quality of all the earth's ecosystems and its resources. The net quality of all of these provides the limiting context and confines to design because our designed system's existence is determined by and dependent upon the demands that it makes on this environmental context. We can state briefly that all our built systems exist because the environment is used as a spatial environment, as an environment for receiving the residues associated with each process, as an environment for providing certain ecological processes, and as an environmental source of material and energy inputs. All these factors are interdependent in that these external ecological dependencies affect the built environment and its functioning, and they in turn are affected by the designed system. We can contend that they form the baseline for all design activity and that in the ecological approach, it is essential for the designer to determine the external ecological dependencies of the proposed design and to find out the probable demands and impacts that the proposed designed system will have upon them.

Every action and activity that takes place in the life cycle of a designed system will have some form of spatial (areal) and systemic impact on the environment because each activity takes place spatially in an ecosystem. The designer's responsibility should therefore include an examination of the ecosystem in which each action and activity takes place spatially, and a determination of the response of that ecosystem to these changes. In many instances, it has been found that much of the damage that has already been inflicted on the existing ecosystem is due to designer's lack of knowledge about the structure and functioning of the ecosystem and its stability prior to any building construction or any human action and activity imposed on it. One of the external ecological dependencies of the built environment is therefore on the spatial zone on which it is located and on which the activities during its life cycle take place (Knowles, 1974; Austin, 1984).

Ecological Description of a Locality

Before the designer can determine the direct ecological spatial impacts of an activity, proposed built structure, or intended change to an ecosystem, an ecological description of the area must first be carried out. This must become an essential part of the designer's site analysis, particularly in the case of a pristine or largely undisturbed, seminatural location. The description would need to be a spatial description (e.g., areal mapping) as well as a systemic description (e.g., measurement of changes over time). As we have described earlier, the ecology of any locality is a complex interaction of the ecosystem's biotic and abiotic components functioning as a whole. In order for the designer to identify the environmental components and processes that are affected by a human action or activity, it is convenient to classify the range of ecosystem factors into features that can be studied separately, e.g., elevation, soils, drainage, microclimate, aspects of vegetation, and so on. Each of these factors can be studied and mapped individually, with different emphasis depending on the locality and the ecosystem. For example, with terrestrial ecosystems, the controlling factors are usually microclimate, available organisms, and geological materials, where the last term includes parent material, relief, and groundwater (e.g., Van Dyne, 1966). Time is also considered as a dimension within which the controlling factors are partially or entirely independent of one another. Each of the controlling factors is a composite of many separate elements, and each element is a variable in time or space.

Operationally, each controlling factor may be considered a multiple-dimensioned matrix. Each change, whether naturally occurring or man-made, is a controlling agent in the ecosystem which produces, in time, a corresponding change in the dependent elements of the ecosystem. The dependent factors in the ecosystem are soils, the primary producers (vegetation), consumer organisms (herbivores and carnivores), decomposer organisms (bacteria, fungi, etc.) and microclimate. Each of these factors is dynamically dependent on the others, and each is a product of the controlling agents through time.

A model that is commonly used for identifying the components and processes of a locality's ecosystems (viz., used in land use planning) is the horizontal "layer-cake" model (McHarg, 1969a, b) (see Fig. 4-1 for a schematic model). This model con-

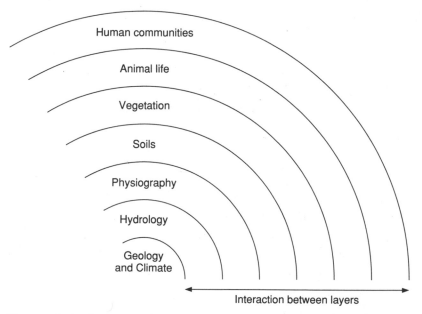

Figure 4-1. A structural "layer-cake" model of the ecosystem.

ceives of the ecology of a locality as a set of levels of components with their own complexities, organizations, and interactions. The components are described under categories such as climate, bedrock and surficial geology, physiography and land forms, ground- and surface-water hydrology, pedology (soils), flora, fauna, and man-made elements. The phenomena in each of these categories are variable. That is to say, for every location these are more or less stressful climatic conditions, there are rock minerals of differing strengths and productivities, there is vegetation comprising communities with distinct values, and there are fauna. Over these phenomena, people have imposed their man-made environment, i.e., the built structures, agricultural systems, and the like. Generally, each level or levels of the model represent a time sequence of ecological development as well as a functional relationship, so that each layer is formed by the interaction and evolution of the preceding layers. It should be noted that human intervention may result in the removal of all the layers down to the geological bedrock (e.g., in a wholly excavated building site).

This structural separation of the layers is done here for the purpose of analysis. The designer must be aware that all these layers are closely related by processes, and that the functioning of one component is determined by its relationship with others. The model in Fig. 4-2 indicates the general pathways of interrelation or influence among the phenomena that were separated in the layer-cake model. (The arrows in this model indicate the directions of influence, many of which are reciprocal.) These two models provide a formal structure for a

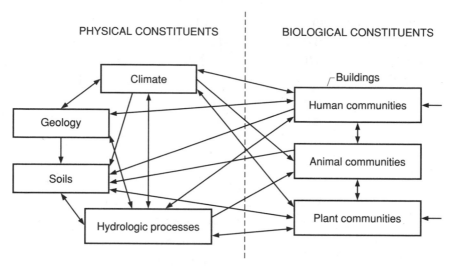

Figure 4-2. Interactions between physical constituents and biological constituents. Many of the linkages are reciprocal.

locality's ecological features. Each of these features can be mapped, inventoried, or otherwise modeled in a variety of ways depending on the designer and the design intentions. For instance, soils may be classified and mapped in different ways depending on how the information is to be used (e.g., agricultural productivity, foundation loading, similarities of parent material, or surface texture differences). For each of the factors shown in the model, its subinteractions should also be considered. For instance, the soil profile of a locality results from the local interaction of edaphic factors over time (climate, parent material, physiography, drainage conditions, and organisms including man) (Hey and Perrin, 1960). To demonstrate the complexity of the subinteractions, the interrelationship of the determining factors in soils is shown in Fig. 4-3.

In examining the ecology of the project site, the designer should be simultaneously aware of the

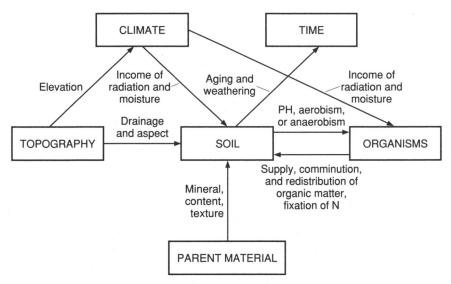

Figure 4-3. Edaphic factors in an ecosystem.

dynamism of the ecosystem and of ecological changes in relationships over seasons. The description of any ecological phenomenon as part of the site analysis is complicated by the fact that being a process, it is in motion. Every ecosystem is modified by the passage of time; the changes in the habitat lead to the emergence of new life forms as organisms' ranges are extended, contracted, or qualified (Elton, 1968). An adequate form of ecosystem monitoring might need to be established for ecosystems with complex interactions and diverse susceptible species, if the changes inflicted on them are of a severe nature.

Although in the layer-cake model the processes and phenomena have been described as discrete components (or layers), we should note that together, all these factors make up the ecosystem of the locality. Each of these factors has specific design and planning implications for the designed system's siting, layout, and pattern of built form. In site analysis, the designer has traditionally considered only the site's topography, drainage, elevation, wind conditions, sun angles, and adjoining structures. However, with the ecological approach, he or she would now have to include in the site analysis a total examination of the ecosystem's controlling factors and processes as a whole system. Furthermore, each action and activity occurring during the life cycle of a designed system will have an impact on the ecosystem in which it took place. In a rigorous analysis of the ecological impacts of a designed system, all these impacts will have to be taken into account.

Essentially, the objectives of such an ecosystem analysis would be to enable the designer to predict the ecosystem's response to the proposed designed action or activity (and/or to assess the consequence of an activity), and not merely to describe the ecosystem. The most common technique used in the analysis review of the information collected using the layer-cake model is the "sieve-map" method. However, a more comprehensive analysis of the ecosystem's functioning would include measurements of the energy flows, nutrient cycling, population dynamics, and other species relationships in the system over time. Other data which must be collected include indirect measurements such as the physical factors associated with biological change (e.g., climate) and direct measurements such as organism growth rates, changes in population densities, and the seasonality of life history events (e.g., reproduction, hibernation, growth period, etc.). These are more accurate indicators of environmental conditions in an ecosystem. Because of year-to-year variations, all these factors should be measured over seasons, and the designed structure should be related to these factors.

Generally, the determination of the type of data and the extent of detail of the data on the external ecological environment depends on the type of action to be imposed upon the ecosystem and on the design program in question. We should note that other models for describing ecosystem features may also be used.

The Dependence by the Built Environment on the Earth as a Supplier of Energy and Material Resources

The physical substance and form of the present built environment are constructed from the renewable and nonrenewable energy and material resources which are derived from the earth's mantle and its ambient environment. In addition to its dependencies upon the ecosystems, the built environment is also dependent for its continued existence upon the earth as a supplier of these energy and material resources. The resources can be classified in many ways, e.g., according to their sources of origin: forest products, nonmetallic minerals and their products, products of a single metal, miscellaneous products, and compound products. We should note that behind each element used in the built environment lies a history of consumption of energy and materials, emission of pollutants, and degradation of ecosystems that has taken place in order to make that particular element available for use in the built environment.

By convention, the sources of energy and materials from the earth are termed natural resources, according to human exploitation patterns. Natural resources are further classified according to their availability and regenerability (Skinner, 1969; Flawn, 1970; Common, 1973). The distinction between replaceable and irreplaceable resources is the "appreciation of their relative importance in relation to the variables which constitutes environment"; this is held by some to be basic to the ecological approach to resource conservation (Costin, 1959). A simple arrangement of these external dependencies of the built environment is as follows:

- *Inexhaustible resources.*   Examples are air, water, and solar energy. Although the total amount of each of these is considered to be virtually inexhaustible, the form in which they occur is subject to change, particularly with respect to their suitability for living systems. Any permanent deleterious change in their composition (e.g., by pollution) is therefore a matter of concern.

- *Replaceable and maintainable resources.*   Examples include water in place and flora and fauna populations. The concept of replaceable and maintainable resources, stated in its simplest terms, means that the production of these resources is primarily a function of the environment, and if environmental conditions are suitable, the resource in question will continue to be produced. Conversely, the impairment of the environment will result in reduced production of the resource. The time profile of the stock depends on many factors, including the deliberate and nondeliberate interference of humanity.

- *Irreplaceable resources.* Examples include minerals, soil, fossil fuels, land, and landscape in the pristine condition. These resources are generally considered irreplaceable in relation to the rate and type of human exploitation. Nonreplaceable energy resources are essentially the past receipts of solar energy and hence have a finite total stock available for depletion. People's present use of these resources is at such a rate that natural regeneration rates are negligible by comparison. Hence there is a sharp intergeneration allocation problem: the more that is used now, the less there will be available for the future.

We must be aware that although the above categorization is useful for some purposes, the categories can change in space and time as new substitutes are found or as the techniques for extraction and recovery change, thus affecting their supply (O'Riordan, 1971).

A further classification of common irreplaceable resources, based on use (Skinner, 1969), is as follows:

- Metallic Mineral Resources

    Abundant metals: iron, aluminum, chromium, manganese, titanium, magnesium

    Scarce metals: copper, lead, zinc, tin, tungsten, gold, silver, platinum, uranium, mercury, molybdenum

- Nonmetallic Mineral Resources

    Minerals for chemical fertilizers and special uses: sodium, chloride, phosphates, nitrates, sulfur, etc.

    Mainly building use: cement, sand, gravel, gypsum, asbestos, etc.

    Water: lakes, rivers, groundwater

- Energy Resources

  Limited and nonrenewable energy sources: fossil fuels,
  e.g., coal, oil, natural gas, oil shale; materials
  capable of nuclear fission or fusion

  Continuous-flow energy sources: primary (solar energy by direct receipt), secondary (solar-energied
  phenomena)

  Examples of direct utilization:
  - Down-flow of precipitated water
  - Tidal response of water
  - Geothermal
  - Wind pressure
  - Climate energy

  Examples of indirect utilization through combus-
  tion, etc.:
  - Photosynthesized energy (e.g., wood)
  - Waste products used as fuel

The fact that the earth contains finite quantities of
the nonrenewable materials and energy resources cannot be disputed. However, what does arouse disagree-
ment among resource conservationists is the question
of quantities: how much of which materials there are,
where they are, how much can be extracted and how
long they will last (e.g., McHale, 1972; Kahn, 1978).
Because the earth and the biosphere are a closed materials system, there obviously are finite limits to the
present state of continuous and increasing human consumption. Virtually all mineral deposits, whether
fuels, metals, or others, have taken geological time for
their formation, and people are consuming them faster
than they are being naturally regenerated. As the
increasing pressure on mineral and fuel resources
leads to the use of lower-grade resources, the problem

of resources depletion can be temporarily dealt with only at the expense of increasing the problems of pollution and ecosystem degradation.

The immediate concern with resource depletion is focused on human and technological limitations rather than geological ones. In some cases the depletion of a resource (e.g., a metal) is governed not so much by the amount of the resource that is needed as by the value placed on it, and this subsequently determines its potential for recovery.

The availability of resources at any particular time is the result of the interaction among the nature and size of human requirements, the physical occurrence of the resource, and the economic cost of extracting, producing, and recovering it. This is further related to people's standard of living and the extent of the patterns of needs that they demand.

However, what is generally agreed is that some form of conservation is necessary in design. In order to maintain the potential choice of uses, rational patterns of utilization need to be designed which would at once conserve the resource and provide resilience and flexibility for future use. The built environment cannot be considered a stable system unless there is a guarantee that the resources on which it depends will continue to be available. To ensure stability, the built environment must be designed to minimize consumption of these resources and to minimize waste, to optimize use, to be more dependent on the "renewable" and "recoverable" (and not the "irrecoverable"). Our design objectives should be to conserve the resource and to provide the potential and flexibility for its future use through design.

Dependence on the Systemic Abilities of the Ecosystems to Assimilate the Discharges from the Built Environment

The built environment as an open system emits outputs in the form of waste discharges into the ecosystems (whether solid, liquid, gaseous, particulate, or others). Some of these outputs are returned to the built environment for recycling and reuse. Others are discharged into the external environment so that they can be assimilated into the ecosystem. The built environment is dependent on its external ecological environment to assimilate its unrecycled waste outputs.

These outputs must find a place in the cycles of the ecosystems, whether with or without some degree of pretreatment or preparation by the designer to facilitate assimilation. For example, local meteorology limits the amount of wastes which can be diluted and carried away by air. The local surface-water flow, rainfall, and runoff limit and determine the amount of wastes which can be discharged into streams, rivers, lakes, and estuaries. The local soil characteristics determine land disposal of wastes, use of groundwater, and application of groundwater recharge for wastewater reclamation. The local topography determines the risk of floods, erosion, and the possibility of use for solid-waste landfill. If the designer is to avoid ecosystem degradation, the output loads of the built environment (during its life cycle) must be kept within the assimilative capacity of the ecosystem and its components. In order to do this, the designer requires, first, detailed knowledge and inventory of the outputs emitted by the designed system and, second, detailed knowledge of the behavior of the biological, chemical, and physical cycles in the ecosystem. Thus, the designer must determine the ecosystem's assimilative capacity and threshold, i.e., an ecosystem description of the locality. Generally stated, most ecosystems have a certain ability to assimilate the outputs from the built environment. However, once this ability is exceeded, the ecosystem will become permanently impaired.

In pollution control, for example, certain indicators of the levels of permissible pollutants are often used to determine the assimilative capacity of the ecosystem. Such indicators, for instance, include:

Form of pollution	Indicators
Water pollution	Algae blooms
	Dissolved oxygen
	Evaporation
	Fecal oliforms
	Nutrients
	Pesticides, herbicides, defoliants
	pH
	Physical water characteristics
	Sediment load
	Stream flow
	Temperature
	Total dissolved solids
	Toxic dissolved solids
	Turbidity
Air pollution	Carbon monoxide
	Hydrocarbon
	Particulate matter
	Photochemical oxidants
	Sulfur oxide
Land pollution	Land use and misuse
	Soil erosion
	Soil pollution

While these indicators are categorized in terms of the three zones (water, air, land), the effects of the pollutants on the ecosystem as a whole should not be neglected. The impacts of these discharges on the biotic factors such as species and populations, habitats and communities, and ecosystem functioning and processes should also be examined.

The type, form, and quantity of the output emitted from the designed system ultimately depend on the design itself, which is further dependent on the interpretation of the specifications of the design program given to the designer. Thus, if a built system can be designed to have minimal emissions of destructive outputs, then it will conserve and at the same time make little use of the assimilative capacity of the ecosystem in which it is located. (The management of output is discussed in Chap. 7.)

Differences between Urban Locations and Greenfield Locations

The importance of each ecological feature of a project site to the designer depends on the ecological condition and importance of the site, which is further dependent upon the geographical location of the site, the complexity and diversity of the ecosystem, and the extent of previous human intervention. Ecological site criteria, as discussed earlier, are generally applicable to nonurban landscapes. The risk of ecosystem degradation as a result of the erection of built systems may be high for certain locations and lower in others.

On an ecologically diverse project site, as in a rural location, building activity and the clearing of vegetation could have the following effects on the biotic components: wide destruction of fragile habitats; direct extermination of species; disturbances to the habitats, causing excessive competition; and reduction of plant cover, with the elimination of some species and the modification of the growth form of others. In such localities, design should be preceded by a comprehensive ecosystem inventory and analysis. However, in locations which have been previously completely built up or which are surrounded by urban developments (as in an urban infill site), it is probable that the ecosystem has been so extensively simplified in its biotic components that mainly the abiotic components of the locality remain and have possible influences on design (e.g., climate, soils, bedrock geology, water regime).

The collection by the designer of ecological data on a project site, to enable a detailed evaluation of impacts, takes time and will incur costs. Sometimes, a complete analysis of an ecosystem may require the measurement of processes over different seasons. In the case of project sites whose locations are ecologically diverse, an ecosystem-based analysis might, for instance, place more emphasis on the plant and animal communities of the planning area as indicators of the ecological condition of the site. This is partly because a complete analysis of the exact nature of the complex interrelationships is a massive undertaking and because the biotic communities can be a fairly accurate reflection of the total effect of all of the environmental influences (Kaiser et al., 1974). By delineating and describing plant communities, an ecologist familiar with the area can derive an approximation of the conditions of the surficial geology, soils, microclimate, hydrologic regimes, and animal community likely to be present. The state of succession of a stand of vegetation would give an indication of the length of time since it was disturbed, and its productivity, ecological diversity, and stability. These parameters, in turn, would indicate the relationships of the community to those around it and the role it plays in the total ecosystem. On this basis, the designer can determine a locality's suitability for an activity or land use, or its susceptibility to serious disruption from various types of land use or building activity. A simplified approach to the layer-cake model is to (1) identify species associations and describe the distribution and abundance of major plant communities, (2) relate species and community distribution to significant physical and biological processes, (3) attempt to assign relative importance values to species and communities based on their significance to major natural processes to be maintained, and (4) make design and planning decisions that minimize permanent biotic changes, multiple effects, and irreversible physical landscape alterations. It must be emphasized that these biotic factors should be used only as an indication of the operation of the other components of the ecosystem; a complete ecosystem analysis, in contrast, would examine the other processes as well and attempt to make the relationship between them and the biotic communities more explicit.

For instance, we can categorize ecological factors into (1) species and populations, (2) habitats and communities, and (3) ecosystems processes as general indicators for ecosystem analysis.

These ecological factors include:

1. Species and populations
   Rare and endangered plant and animal species
   Productive plant species
   Game species
   Other animals
   Resident and migratory birds
   Pestilent plant and animal species
   Parasites
2. Habitats and communities
   Species diversity
   Food chains
   Land use for habitats and communities
3. Ecosystem processes
   Productive rate
   Hydrological rate
   Nutrient rate

These factors do not imply the weighting of one consideration over another. Among ecologists and biologists, there are philosophical differences concerning which components of the ecosystem need to be protected against human modification. For instance, one approach may be to preserve an unaltered ecosystem and another to protect all the organisms within the ecosystem. It is also probable that both approaches may be valid. Each locality has to be assessed individually in the light of its environmental context and the designer's priorities.

Design Strategies

Following from the examination by the designer of the ecology of a location in which an activity will take place spatially, the design and planning task now becomes one of determining the extent of impact that can or cannot be permitted on that ecosystem as a result of the spatial displacement of the ecosystem by the designed system, by the activities associated with the designed system, and by the operations of the designed system during its life span.

The designer must ensure that as long as the impacts on an ecosystem are kept within the threshold of the ecosystem (i.e., by temporary changes), it can recover, given time, and subsequent large-scale degradation of the ecosystem will not be brought about. However, once certain biotic communities and their species have been intentionally obliterated, they cannot be reinstated easily. It is generally easier to protect an existing ecosystem than to restore it after it has been cleared. Succession, change, and resiliency in ecosystems are interrelated (Holling and Goldberg, 1973). When a large area is stripped of its vegetation, a historical process begins that leads to the evolution of a mature ecosystem through a series of successional stages. For example, this process of recovery is restricted and halted by the act of paving over the area with an impervious surface.

In biological conservation, it is held that within an ecologically diverse site (as in a pristine ecosystem), there are irreplaceable components whose value can be measured only in the long run through their long-term contribution to the stability of the biosphere (Dasman, 1968). The features of the ecosystems thus represent biological and physical parameters within which the technical and spatial features of the built environment should be designed. The designer must first have a clear understanding of the design objectives and the full range of actions and activities associated with the design. After this, an awareness of the ecosystem's parameters would give him or her an indication of the ecological importance of the project site and which interventions it can permit, and an indication of which features can be modified and which cannot. The design efforts would then be adapted to fit within the constraints, restraints, and opportunities of the ecosystem. In ecologically important and diverse locations, these parameters should be examined in detail before any change to the ecosystem is made. Following this, the changes should be executed only with an adequate monitoring of the system response to ensure that nothing in the existing order is permitted to become permanently lost or impaired as a result of human activity unless all foreseeable consequences have been considered and the appropriate preventive action has been taken.

In the ecological design process, the designer must inventory the total set of actions and activities in each stage of the designed system's life cycle. Within each stage in the life cycle for each activity that takes place, the following questions must be asked regarding the ecosystem that is affected:

- What environments in the project area are affected by the activity, and how are these environments characterized?
- How do these environments change physically and chemically with the activity?
- What species are involved: aquatic, terrestrial, and marine?

- Considering the environments and species that can be identified, what ecological processes are at work causing changes that result from the activity?
- Knowing the ecological processes at work, what ecological changes can be anticipated?

In general, design decisions should be made with the goal of minimizing (1) the permanent changes on the biotic community, (2) multiple and far-reaching effects that may influence other ecosystems, and (3) extreme physical alteractions of the ecosystem that may have irreversible effects.

Before detailed design, in the layout planning stages of the built environment, an examination of the ecological features of the project site (or location of the intended activity) will provide the designer with a basis for making the following design decisions (Wettqvst et al., 1971):

- The type of land use pattern, or the exclusion of certain structures and activities from ecologically unsuitable locations. This would include areas which are hazardous to built structures.
- Preservation areas, or the determination of areas having particular value in their existing state for preservation (i.e., the spontaneous state of the ecosystem is preserved). This concept includes considerations of ecologically sensitive flora and fauna and fragile topographical features peculiar to the region.
- Conservation areas, or the determination of areas having particular value in their existing state for conservation. These localities are not ecologically

critical but could provide buffer zones for preservation areas and represent a retention of future use options.

- Siting and planning layout pattern, or the seeking of compatible siting combinations of ecosystem components and man-made components. Locations suitable for man-made structures include areas already developed, undeveloped areas now vacant or used for other purposes that are suitable for intensive development, and undeveloped areas with some physical limitations (e.g., drainage problems, poor permeability, salt-water intrusion). In general, the areas suitable for building are those not considered ecologically fragile. Within such areas, further delineation might be necessary to prevent building over lands which are intrinsically agriculturally productive.

- Impacts during the life cycle of the designed system and the exclusion of other structures and activities during and after the construction of a designed system so that the impacts on the ecosystems could be kept within tolerance levels.

We should note that the impact of each intended activity also changes over time, as recovery within the ecosystem itself can sometimes be effected. The overall impact of a designed system on an ecosystem might range from a minimal intervention into the location's ecology to a permanent degradation of the ecosystem. For instance, an activity may have the following negative levels of effects:

- Disturb the ecosystems by temporary change (e.g., by a batch disposal of sewage wastes into a stream)

- Disfigure the ecosystem by a surface change (e.g., by a slight change in topography)
- Disrupt the ecosystem by a permanent change (e.g., by a complete clearing of the ecosystem's biotic substrate down to its bedrock)

A designed system does not have only negative impacts on the ecosystems. In designing for compatible relations with the ecosystems, the designed system may have positive relationships which

- Preserve the ecosystem (e.g., nature reserve management)
- Enhance the ecosystem by adding value to it as a resource (e.g., rehabilitation of derelict sites)
- Retard environmental deterioration by reducing the existing trend of change (e.g., the changing of an erosion inducing drainage)
- Restore the ecosystem by replacing existing designed conditions (e.g., the revegetation of derelict land)

The external ecological interdependencies of the built environment and how they may be incorporated in the design process are as follows:

1. The external ecological interdependencies of the built environment consist of the totality of all the earth's ecosystems and resources.
2. An awareness of the features of the ecosystems on which human activities are to be imposed provides baseline criteria prior to the introduction of major changes. Where the impact of a designed system or an intended activity on the ecosystem could cause

detrimental changes, the implementation of the action should be weighed against the preventive or corrective measures that could be incorporated into the design and the other possible alternative design solutions. An ecosystem can be described in a number of ways. A method commonly used in land use planning is the layer-cake method.

3. The impacts of all the interdependencies of the built environment on the earth's ecology and resources should be considered in the design process. For instance, the provision of inputs into a built system, the emission of outputs from a built system, and the operational activities within a built system all have impacts on the components and processes of the ecosystems on which they take place spatially. Furthermore, the impacts on the project site's ecosystem and on other affected ecosystems over the life cycle of the designed system should also be anticipated.

4. At the outset, an awareness of the effects on the ecosystems of the project site would facilitate future computation of the ecological consequences of other intended built environments and provide a basis for minimizing undesirable future changes to the ecological environment.

5. The built environment is also dependent on its external environment as a supplier of energy and materials resources for its physical form and substance as well as for maintaining its operations. If the long-term supply of these resources is to be ensured, then a conservation approach to their use should become a design criterion. Immediate design objectives should be to provide flexibility for future use.

6. The ecosystems also act as a sink to assimilate discharges from the built environment. The ability of an ecosystem to assimilate by these discharges is limited. If the threshold is exceeded, the ecosystem will become permanently impaired. Design should ensure that minimum outputs are discharged and that they are kept within the assimilative capacity of the ecosystem, or else contribute positively to the functioning of the ecosystem.

7. As one ecosystem is interconnected to other ecosystems within the biosphere, it is important to ensure that one action on an ecosystem (which may not have immediately apparent impact on that location) does not have detrimental impacts on ecosystems elsewhere. The importance of the impact of any human action on the ecology of the project site will depend on the ecological condition and value of that ecosystem and on the type of action that is to be inflicted on the ecosystem.

In an earlier chapter we mentioned that the designer must analyze the ecosystem on which the project site is located before imposing any action upon it. In this chapter, we described some of the methods and indicators that may be used in ecosystem analysis as part of the designer's site investigations. In the site planning for a built environment, an ecosystem analysis of the project site will provide the designer with a basis for determining the type of land use, preservation areas, conservation areas, siting, and built-form patterns and impacts during the life cycle of the designed system.

In the selection and design of the built system's form and servicing systems, the task is to seek compatible and positive relations between the operational interactions of the designed system and the project ecosystems.

The life cycle of any designed system should be examined stage by stage using the interactions framework to check the impacts on the ecosystems of each action and activity incurred in that stage.

5
Internal Ecological Interdependencies of the Built Environment

Internal Interdependencies

The internal ecological interdependencies of the built environment consist of the external ecological impacts and interactions that result from the entire set of actions and activities of the designed system during its life cycle. These interdependencies include the spatial displacement impacts on the ecosystems, the extent of energy and material inputs used by the designed system, the emissions of energy and material outputs, and the influences of human actions and activities that take place in the use of the built environment. In total, the ecological interactions caused by the built environment are not

simply those inherent in the making and building of
the built structures, but include also all the environmental interactions that arise from the use of the
built structures, their disposal, and their recovery.

We can consider these internal ecological interdependencies of the built environment conceptually as
a form of energy and materials management. In
order to understand its impact we can structure it in
the form of specific patterns of use of energy and
materials, flowing from the environmental sources
of origin through the built environment and eventually ending up in their environmental sinks. In this
way, we would be able to examine all built structures in terms of their own individual patterns of
use, and anticipate, by means of design efforts, the
extent of the demands and impacts that this pattern
will make on the earth's ecosystems and its
resources. The set of actions and activities that take
place within the life cycle of a designed system is
related to and interdependent with the flow of
inputs into the built environment, the discharge of
outputs from the built environment, and the limitations of the earth's ecosystems and resources.

The Economic Life and Physical Life of a Building Element

In analyzing the use of energy and materials in a
designed system as a pattern of use, we can consider a built system and its subelements to possess a
specific life span within the biosphere. We may further draw a distinction between its physical life and
its economic life.

The economic life of a built system is generally considered to be that period during which it produces a financial income adequate to justify the investment involved (or, in the case of an owner-occupied building, that period during which it is in direct use) (Weimer and Hoyt, 1966). Although this is considered to be distinct from a built system's physical life, there is an apparent relationship between the physical life and the period during which satisfactory economic returns are received. The physical life of a built system is that period of time during which that built system remains in use in the built environment before it is assimilated and introduced into the ecosystems. We should note that presently designers tend to be more concerned with the economic life than the physical life. However, in the ecological approach, the physical life of a designed system is more important.

At present, for instance, buildings have been financed and designed in the expectation that they will last for around thirty years (their estimated economic life), after which they are considered valueless (Crosby, 1973, p. 9). In practice, most of the present stock of buildings, by virtue of its long-lasting form of construction, is capable of outliving the investment period. Since the buildings' reuse within the built environment was not anticipated by design at the outset, they become thoroughly inconvenient and inadequate for subsequent reuse and renewal.

Generally, the physical life is longer than the economic life. For example, the life span for some construction systems (e.g., reinforced concrete frame, stonework, glass) far exceeds their designed economic life. A component part of a built system or even the entire built system may be dispensed with or demolished for a number of reasons; for instance:

- *Locational obsolescence.* The use for which it was originally designed and built may no longer be appropriate in that particular location.
- *Functional obsolescence.* Social or economic changes may remove the demand for the services and functions provided in or by the built system.
- *Technical obsolescence.* Design and technological developments may raise performance standards beyond those which the built system can satisfy.
- *Physical obsolescence.* The built system and its components may fall below acceptable standards required by the occupants or statutory regulations as a result of the physical forces of deterioration, weathering, and decomposition by the action of the ecological environment.

However, at the end of the intended economic life, the physical life of the building element persists. In order to avoid excessive discharges of wastes into the ecosystems at the end of the built system's economic life, there should be some form of extension of the use of the building element so that it remains within the built environment. In the ecological approach, if we are to consider synoptically the use of materials and energy by the built environment and its users, then every element in the designed system must be evaluated not only in its economic context but also in its ecological context in terms of its physical life and the route that it takes during its life span.

Design Responsibility for the Long-Term Fate of the Built System

At present, designers are not responsible (legally or otherwise) for the disposal of the elements of the designed system after completion of construction. The long-term ecological fate of their products is not traditionally considered to be their responsibility.

Very often, at the end of a built system's designed life, it is demolished and the building materials are thrown away or relocated somewhere else. The flow in the present economic system is a one-way process based on the concept of taking natural resources from the earth, changing and assembling them into goods, selling them to the consumer, and then forgetting about them. The consumer uses the product (in this case, a building) but he or she does not consume it—he or she just discards it after using it. The products that have traditionally been labeled "consumed" in fact render temporary service within the built environment, after which the physical substances remain and eventually become outputs to the ecological environment in the form of waste products.

To repeat our earlier premise, if the materials and energy that are used in the built system are to be seen holistically as part of the biosphere's continuum of flows and processes, then any built structure in use is simply in a phase in its life cycle when the energy and materials have been locked into that particular form of use. At the end of its life in that form of use, it is transferred to another phase in its life cycle, e.g., as a waste product or as a reused element. Waste includes both the residuals from production processes and the product itself after it has served its useful life. Should this one-way flow continue, the widespread discarding of building wastes would result in accumulation in the ecosystem and subsequent stresses on the ecological environment. Any element that does not contribute to the problem of disposal of outputs when it is in use, does so when it is discarded. From the viewpoint of the disposal of waste products, existing architecture and built structures are in effect potential waste products whose reuse needs design efforts.

In the ecological approach, the designer's awareness of and responsibility for any product must therefore extend to what happens to it after it is placed in the hands of the consumer (or the users of the built environment). Ideally, in a rigorous ecological approach, the designer must be able to specify not only how and at what environmental cost (in the form of demands and impacts on the earth) a designed system could be built but also how and at what environmental cost it is used, managed, and disposed of afterward. In order to do this, the use of energy and materials in the built environment might be better conceived as a form of *management of their patterns of use*.

Linear and Cyclical Patterns of Use of Materials

We identify here two basic patterns of use—the linear and the cyclical pattern. The existing pattern of use of materials in the man-made environment is basically a linear pattern or a "once-through" flow of nonrenewal (i.e., from resource to use to waste). This pattern amounts to a linear transformation of resources into wastes with a brief period of use in between (Davoll, 1971, p. 335), after which the wastes then pose problems of disposal and contamination. As rare materials become depleted by this linear pattern of nonrenewal it becomes crucial that some form of conservation of use be exercised.

For instance, a conservation strategy would be to extend the useful life span of a processed material by widespread large-scale recovery. It is obviously wasteful to use mineral resources (particularly metallic minerals) only once, especially when they have been laboriously located, processed, and transported at the cost of high energy use and ecosystem degradation. The disposal of one product after use also means that another must be produced to replace it. This almost invariably means the depletion of more resources and the need for more expenditure of energy resources elsewhere, besides also creating a disposal problem. In some cases, just extending the life of a built system will only delay the disposal problems. The initial and terminal environmental impact of the disposal of a durable product may exceed that of a poorer-quality product that needs more frequent replacement.

If all the man-made products could be recovered (through reuse, regeneration, and recycling) at the minimum cost of resource inputs, it would lessen the overall demands on nonreplaceable resources. The management of renewable resources would also be less intensive as demand for their production would be reduced. Since the earth's material and fossil energy resources have finite limits, it becomes

increasingly essential that major advances be made
to recover the used materials, to minimize waste,
and to curtail as much as possible the use of the
irrecoverable resources. Many discharges which
have caused pollution could be more appropriately
considered "resources out of place" if their recovery
could be effected. In order to facilitate recovery, we
require a cyclical pattern of use of energy and materials in the built environment.

The advantages of having a cyclical pattern of use
of materials are:

- To reduce the problems of output disposal
- To conserve the earth's resources
- To reduce environmental contamination as a dis-
posal problem
- To reduce the throughput of energy and material
resources by the built environment

If the designer were able to ensure that the loop in
the pattern of use from natural resource to product
to user to another resource is made to close cyclically, so that an element once used is returned into the
system, then an ideal solution would be
approached. What had been a residual or a discard
would now be remade or redesigned into another
resource. In effect, the objective of conservation of
natural resources may be seen in its broadest sense
as the effort to make a cyclical process more cyclical
(Odum, E. P., 1971).

However, we should acknowledge that a completely cyclical pattern of use is an ideal system and
is not achievable in absolute terms. For instance,

there will always be an intrinsic loss in each recovery cycle. In the case of scrap steel recycling, there is an approximately 10 percent loss in each cycle. Furthermore, not all materials can be recirculated. For example, such materials as paints, thinners, solvents, and cleaners cannot perform their function without being dissipated into the environment. There are also losses from all processes (including recovery processes), e.g., friction and oxidation losses. Even in a hypothetical system in which total recovery and recycling are practiced, the energy requirements for recovery and reprocessing of residuals would inevitably produce an unavoidable residual, thermal emission. Taking the premise that a cyclical pattern of use is preferable to a linear pattern, then the recovery potential of any built structure must be consciously designed for at the outset. However, predesigning the recovery potential into a designed system will incur additional environmental costs and interactions, which must be taken into account to ensure that they will not introduce additional environmental problems.

Patterns of Use of Energy and Materials in a Model Ecosystem and Their Design Implications

It is worthwhile to draw an analogy here between the flow of energy and materials in a model ecosystem and that in the built environment (Yeang, 1972).

The biosphere, in order to maintain itself (and the living systems within), recirculates essential materials in the ecosystems so that after use, they are returned in a reusable form. Thus the biological processes acting on the biosphere might be described broadly as mostly cyclical rather than linear (or "one-way").

The dependence of life on energy flows coincides with a similar dependence on the cyclical flow of materials within the ecosystems (Ovington, 1964; Kormondy, 1969). The rotation of materials in an ecosystem (e.g., the cycling of nutrients) is often given as one of its characteristics (Borman and Liken, 1967; Odum, E. P., 1971). Ecologists hold that these two principles are equally applicable to any level and type of organism and ecosystem (Odum, H. T., 1971). These two principles are represented in the model in Fig. 5-1. In this model of the ecosystem, the various trophic levels, together with the dead materials and the decomposers, are seen as discrete entities represented as boxes. We should note that in a real system, the trophic levels consist of innumerable connections and do not come as discrete compartments. The consumers, producers, and decomposers of ecosystems often have many and changing roles.

Energy enters by the way of the producers, then flows from compartment to compartment and is radiated from the system. Matter is circulated within the system. The *closing of the loop* or the tightening of the biogeochemical cycle in the ecosystem is an important trend in its successional development (Odum, E. P., 1969). Mature ecosystems have a greater capacity to hold nutrients for cycling within the system than developing ones do. Although it is broadly held that the cyclical flow of materials is a fundamental pattern of use of materials in ecosys-

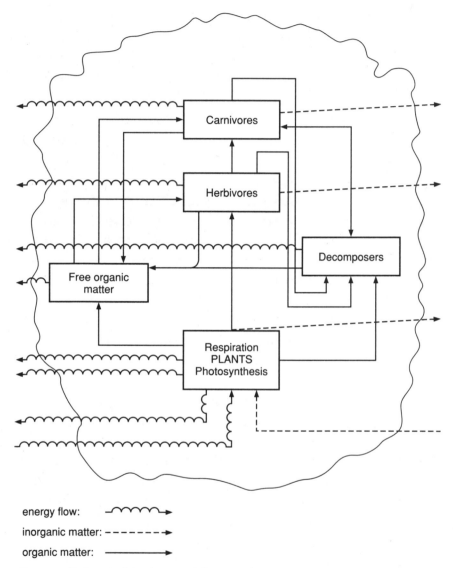

energy flow: ∿∿∿➤

inorganic matter: - - - - - - - ➤

organic matter: ——————➤

Figure 5-1. Model of energy flow and matter cycling in an ecosystem (adapted from Colinvaux, 1973).

tems, in most ecosystems these cycles are always incomplete (Sjors, 1955). The processes are thus cyclical but not completely closed, even though the biosphere acts as a closed resource system.

   The biological structures in the existing built environment in urban ecosystems can be examined using the ecosystem model. An urban ecosystem has a small producer component on which the resident consumers (viz., humans) hardly feed at all. The plants growing in cities play an insignificant role in the total energy flux as compared to those in nonurban situations. The city is a dependent ecosystem operating on energy fixed by external producers (e.g., the agricultural system), both in contemporary rural ecosystems and, more important, in past ecosystems locked up in fossil fuels such as coal and oil (Fraser and Dasman, 1972; Hughes, 1974). The city operates as would a reducer-dominated ecosystem operating on a vastly enhanced flow of imported energy. The urban ecosystem resembles certain aquatic ecosystems such as rivers and oyster reefs, where energy and fluxes are much determined by conditions upstream. This state of affairs leads to an ecosystem whose behavior is much less predictable. In short, ecosystems with broken material cycles are dependent on external events and supplies of inputs.
   We can find another obvious discrepancy in the biological structure of the existing urban ecosystem in its decomposer component. The decomposer component of the urban ecosystem is not an integral part of its biological structure and its capacity is inadequate in relation to that of the other components. Although in the ecosystem model, decomposers are described on one trophic level, the relationship is far more complex. For instance, there are fungi that live on fungi, bacteria, and so on. All of them are in a sense decomposers (Billings, 1964). This trophic level is in effect a collection of several

different trophic levels, all utilizing energy to return re-sources to the environment. The various members of this trophic level also utilize dead plant or animal matter or wastes from all the lower trophic levels. The importance of the decomposer component in the ecosystem is obvious, since without it, dead materials would simply accumulate, and raw materials in short supply (such as phosphorus) would be tied up in the remains of plants and animals. The decomposers provide the necessary cycling mechanism in the ecosystem. Energy flows in at one end of an ecosystem (in photosynthesis) and flows out at the other (by respiration). Because of the decomposers, the elemental materials are recycled to some extent within the system and between systems.

The existing linear pattern of use of materials and energy resources by the man-made environment has resulted in the overall short-circuiting of many of the local and global processes within the biosphere (e.g., entrophication of inland waters, consumption of fossil fuels, etc.).

As we have described earlier, the built environment's dependencies should not be laid entirely on the biosphere's capacity for regeneration of all its outputs. The time scales of the ecological processes of regeneration and of human consumption are presently incompatible. The natural regeneration rates could (and need to) be accelerated by human intervention, provided such intervention does not introduce additional environmental problems. A cyclical pattern of use is essential, preferably one analogous to that in the ecosystem. This means that the decomposer component of the built environment should be of an adequate capacity in comparison to its producer and consumer components. This means that the recovery pattern of the man-made environment must match its own production and use patterns rather than depending completely on the biosphere's processes for assimilation and regeneration.

The Life Cycle of the Built Environment

The cycling of materials in buildings may be represented as a simple cycle with growth and decay as opposites. For instance, most existing cities are at different points in this cycle. Similarly, urban renewal programs are based largely on the state of decay of the existing stock of buildings.

In the existing built environment, waste materials from the demolition of buildings and other processes are usually discarded in an unseparated state. For instance, at present a certain amount of salvage already takes place, and certain parts are recovered as scrap (e.g., bricks and rubble are reused as landfill). About 25 percent of the major material resources consumed are recycled within the built environment (Klaff, 1973).

In a synoptic approach to the use of energy and materials, the management of the energy and materials in the built environment throughout the life cycle of the designed system must be considered by the designer. This remedies the designers' previous erroneous emphasis on only the first costs of the built environment. The actions and activities associated with and within the built environment by its users can be structured using the framework of this cyclical pattern of use.

A cycle can be thought of as a series of transformations (Ashby, 1958). Thus if a subsystem has four clearly recognizable states, a, b, c, and d, and the transformation goes $a–b–c–d–a–b$ and so on, then the sequence of state is cyclical. This can be shown kinematically as (Schultz, 1969):

or, when put on a time scale as a sine wave:

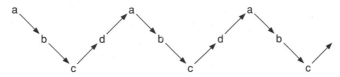

and so on. For instance, the flow of materials in the built environment could go through a cycle of *extraction (or harvest)—transport—processing—use— recycling—and/or disposal*. We can therefore structure a general cycle of activities of a model built environment into the following phases:

1. *Production phase.* This phase consists of the processes and activities involved in the extraction, preparation, and distribution of raw materials and energy forms for use by the built environment.

2. *Construction phase.* This phase consists of the processes and activities that take place spatially upon the site of the built environment. It may include the fabrication of building elements and components, their assembly, all on-site construction actions and processes, the use of on-site

materials and energy forms in construction, and the on-site production processes.

3. *Operational or consumption phase.* This phase consists of the activities and processes of the built environment and its users after the construction of the built environment. These include the operation, maintenance, and subsequent modifications of the built systems and other consumption processes.

4. *Recovery phase.* This phase consists of the activities and processes taken to close the loop in the cycle of use of materials. It includes the removal, demolition, renewal, recycling, reuse, and regeneration processes. This phase might include efforts taken to rehabilitate the site with flora and fauna.

These phases are related together in Fig. 5-2.

We can use this cyclical use pattern to identify the internal ecological interdependencies and impacts of each component of the built environment. The

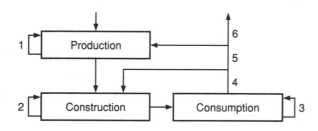

where
1. recovery within production processes
2. recovery of construction residuals for construction processes
3. recovery patterns in consumption
4. recovery of consumption materials into production processes
5. recovery of construction materials into production processes
6. redirect of materials elsewhere

Figure 5-2. A cyclical pattern of use.

model indicates the possible routes along which energy and materials could flow. At each phase we will find that inputs (of other energy and materials) are taken in, outputs are emitted, and each phase takes place spatially on a location upon which it may have detrimental ecological impacts. We can check that all these correlate with the interactions framework (in Chap. 3).

When we consider the use of energy and materials in this way, we are reminded of the other phases in the pattern of use besides the consumption phase. For instance, attention has previously been focused on the production phase, whereas the processes which produced it are often forgotten by designers. Behind each component in the designed system lies a history of consumption of energy and materials, emissions of pollutants, and degradation of ecosystems. Thus, if the ecological implications and interactions of the use of every element in a building are to be made explicit, the designer must trace the history of each element right back to its constituent raw materials and add up all the matter and energy used and waste produced, and the attendant impacts on the ecological environment, at each step of the route. Although each step in the chain might appear to be moderately efficient, the overall picture would show excessive wastage of matter and energy and degradation of the environment. In the present economy, the only coordination involved in the chain has been the economic criteria, which are often unjustifiable on ecological grounds. A breakdown of the life-cycle costs of a built structure in terms of the energy and materials consumed have been approximated in Fig. 5-3.

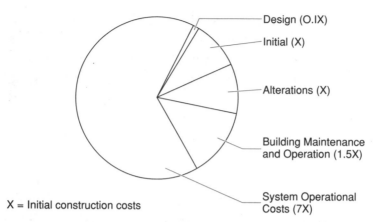

Figure 5-3. Life-cycle energy costs of a built system. We
should note that the system operational costs over its life span
far exceed the costs in its other stages (adapted from Isola,
1973).

The design task should not be directed totally
toward a static equilibrium state in which every-
thing is recirculated and used. This is not achievable
in practice and would not be desirable for all design
situations. In any case, existing buildings are not
made from homogeneous materials but are multi-
component products. Ideally, the design goal should
be a cyclical pattern of use, which will minimize all
wastes and losses from all the activities and processes without introducing additional environmental
problems, minimize the spatial impacts on ecosystems, and retain the stability of the ecosystems.

The Spatial Impact of the Patterns of Use in the Built Environment

As stated earlier, all actions and activities associated
with a designed system should be identified early

on at the design stage for their potential for environmental disruption. We can use a conceptual cyclical pattern for resource management to discover the range of actions and activities that take place in the life cycle of that designed system and to anticipate their likely ecosystem impacts and interactions. Through the course of this analysis, any human action or activity which results in a change (e.g., alteration, addition, depletion) in the components and processes of the ecosystem (in which it takes place spatially) can be regarded as having an environmental impact or interaction.

The bases for this are:

- Each human activity has a basic potential for disruption of the ecosystem.
- A particular activity will tend to have a higher or lower impact relative to other activities.
- The potential for disruption combined with the ecological tolerance of any location will determine the impacts of any action or activity on a specific area.
- The density and intensity of an activity are variables. In some cases these could be considered as other controlling factors in an activity's impact.
- The duration of an activity (e.g., the life span of a built system or period of waste emissions) is also an important variable. Some ecosystems can tolerate a considerable amount of certain activities or uses over a short period of time. It is possible that an activity may be scheduled so as to match it with the tolerance time spans of the areas used.
- The impact of an activity might be affected by the presence of other activities. The interactions and multiple effects should be considered.

Designing for a Cyclical Pattern of Use

The designed system is in effect the result of specific decisions made by the designer regarding the pattern of use of energy and materials in the built environment. Designing for a cyclical pattern of use in the built environment is related to a number of factors, for instance:

1. *The energy and material cost of recovery (viz., a cyclical pattern).* At present, in the design of large-scale buildings, much thought is given to the ease and efficiency of construction (i.e., to the energy required to build the system) and to the efficiency of operation. Little thought is given to what is required to dismantle it. Buildings still tend to be built "permanently," even though the economic life of many of the components grows steadily shorter (McHale, 1967, p. 123). What should be included in the design process is an awareness of the energy and material inputs and wastage to be incurred in the dismantling of a built system and in the preparation of its components for recovery or recirculation. Although, in principle, most materials used in building could be recovered, a complete regeneration of all components cannot be achieved without an additional expenditure of energy and materials. Thus one criterion in determining the use of a material would be the energy and material cost of its later recovery.

2. *The ecosystem impacts of dismantling and recovery.* The impacts on the ecosystem of the processes of demolition, dismantling, removal, and recovery also need to be considered. For instance, the demolition of a building by the use of heavy mechanical equip-

ment may have detrimental effects on the surrounding ecosystem. Some recovery processes may require the setting up of processing plants.

3. *The emissions and outputs of recovery processes.* The emissions and outputs involved in providing the cyclical pattern of use need to be considered. The designer has to ensure that these processes do not introduce additional pollutants into the environment.

4. *The form, type, and mass of materials used in the built system.* The need for material recovery is related to the rarity, abundance, or ease of production of the material in question. For instance, the recovery of gold is considered commonplace because of the monetary value placed on the element. The recovery of aluminum, an abundant element in the biosphere, is considered necessary because of the high energy cost of its production and the lower energy cost of its recovery.

5. *The forms of construction.* The ease of dismantling and recovery depends on the forms of construction and assembling that are used. For instance, steel and other metals used in building could be collected as scrap and melted down for another use. However, reinforced concrete construction, having undergone a chemical reaction, cannot be returned to its separate components of sand and cement (and steel). It can be reused only in a downgraded form (or at a lower potential, e.g., for landfill or for hardcore). Clearly mechanical systems of construction and jointing facilitate recovery more than other types. Physico-chemical systems of construction (e.g., reinforced concrete, cement, and mortar) have a lower recovery potential.

An impermanent structural solution (one that is easily demountable) is generally applicable on a small scale when the timing of removal and recovery can be based on personal standards of habitability and use without the need for a public consensus. Structural parts of large-scale built systems (such as high-rise buildings) tend generally to be permanent, as their requirements for stability, safety, fire protection, etc., inevitably dictate a long-lasting construction system. Various means of structural economies (such as continuity of structural members, in situ and physico-chemical joints, and the use of complex composite components) may be specified at the design and construction phase under the assumption of permanence or for reasons of economic saving. These decisions are made at the expense of ease and economy at the dismantling and salvage stage.

It should be remembered that if the complete recovery of a built system were pursued relentlessly, the result might likely be an oversophisticated and material-redundant structural life-support system for a building. A totally recoverable building system is possible only at the expense of some other criterion, e.g., an added expenditure of energy and materials to facilitate the recovery, the environmental impacts of the recovery processes, or the degree of built-in redundancy of materials used in the built system.

6. *The manner of demolition or dismantling.* The quality of the dismantled building components will depend on the nature of the obsolescence and manner of dismantling that is employed. In order for components to be reused, they must be physically sound or repairable and must be compatible with the new use with regard to dimensions, performance, form, and

method of fixing. Thus one design consideration that would affect the recovery of the built system is the method of demolition or dismantling. This varies according to whether complex components are being recovered or whether individual materials are being salvaged for regeneration. The ability to dismantle effectively is the link between design and construction on the one hand and recovery on the other. In most cases at present, built systems have not been designed adequately for ease of recovery.

7. *The existence of a use or a need for the recovered product.* Designing building systems and components with material recovery in mind would presuppose the continued relevance and use of the product in the future, or its compatibility with future systems. Unless the product relates to something with a universal use (e.g., a brick), the built-in recovery could easily become redundant.

The geographic complexity in the recovery process of the building elements is attributable more to the complexity of the building design, which uses materials from many sources, than to complications in the recovery pattern. For instance, the scrap material may be too low in quantity to be reused, or a market for the recovered product may not exist.

8. *Choice of servicing systems.* The type of environmental (i.e., M&E) servicing systems used to provide the comfort and material requirements of the built environment may be designed to reduce the throughput of energy and materials during the operational phase of the built environment's life. Systems should be selected or designed to be cyclical in nature and to reduce consumption of resources and wastage.

In the ecological approach, the designer's awareness of and responsibility for the designed system should extend to what happens to it after it is placed in the hands of the users. Ideally, in a rigorous approach, the designer must be able to specify not only how and at what environmental cost (in the form of demands and impacts on the earth) a designed system could be built, but also at what environmental cost it is used, managed, and disposed of afterward.

Some of the main considerations are:

- The internal ecological interdependencies of the built environment consist of the ecological impacts or interactions that result from the entire set of actions that take place within or are associated with the life cycle of the designed system.

- The ecological impacts of the built environment are not simply those inherent in the making and building of the built structures, but include the environmental problems that the use of these structures, their disposal, and their recovery generate. We can conceive their impacts in the context of a pattern of use.

- A built element has both an economic life as well as physical life. The physical life by far exceeds the economic life, and the element's disposal is the concern of the environmentalist.

- The designer should be responsible for the designed system not only during its economic life but also during its physical life.

- We can identify two basic patterns of use: the linear pattern and the cyclical pattern. The designer's goal is to ensure that the designed system tends toward a cyclical pattern of use that minimizes resource consumption, minimizes all wastes and losses from the activities and processes without introducing additional environmental problems, minimizes the system's spatial impacts on the ecosystems, and retains the stability of the ecosystems.

- The built environment is a dynamic system which has continuous interactions with its ecological environment. An examination of its ecological impacts during only its construction and operation phases would be incomplete. The interactions that a built system has with its ecological environment occur throughout all the phases of its life cycle. These interactions occur from the point at which materials (and energy forms) are extracted from the biosphere; through their use in the production, construction, and operation phases of the built system; and up to the point when they become residues requiring disposal and recovery. During the life span of each building element and component, other energy and material inputs are also used, and at the same time outputs are emitted. Thus, for a design approach to be termed ecological, it must have a synoptic view of the management and use of materials and energy by a built system. Such a view would include an understanding and assessment of the interactions and impacts of all the actions and activities for all the phases in the life span of a built system. A rigorous ecological approach to the design and planning of the built environment would consider and anticipate the impacts of all the phases in the life cycle.
- The design goal is not to design a built system in which every element and component is recirculated

but to design systems that are efficient in their use of energy and materials in all the phases, do not introduce contaminant outputs, and minimize the spatial impacts on the ecosystems within the biosphere. Thus built systems must be designed not only for their use but also for their recovery and eventual reintegration into the biospheric processes.

- Which aspects of a built system can be recovered and which cannot should be investigated and facilitated early in the design stage.

- It is possible that in order to justify the initial diseconomy encountered in designing a built system as part of a cyclical pattern of use, the recovery potential of the built system might be made a prominent feature of its economic life span. This condition will doubtless increase its availability and effect changes in economic priority.

- The internal interdependencies of the built environment can be conceived in the form of a cyclical pattern of use of energy and materials. The pattern of this can be structured into the following stages in the *life cycle* of a designed system:
  1. Production phase
  2. Construction phase
  3. Operational phase
  4. Recovery phase

This life cycle represents a pattern of use in which the sets of activities associated with a built structure can be related. All design can be carried out within the framework of this cyclical pattern. In this way, the ecological consequences of each activity can be considered holistically.

6

External-to-Internal Ecological Interdependencies of the Built Environment

Transactions between the Designed System and Its Environment

The external-to-internal ecological interdependencies of the built environment and the external-to-internal exchanges from the environment to our designed system consist of those inputs of energy and materials that are directed externally from the environment into our designed system for its realization and operation (including those needed for its maintenance and disposal processes). These include not only the energy and materials used to synthesize its physical substance and form, but also those which are used to operate the built system and to maintain it in all the phases of its entire life cycle (e.g., production, construction, operation, and recovery). Simultaneously, during this process, outputs are also emitted into the environment and other impacts are inflicted upon the ecosystems.

As described earlier, building activity can be seen as a form of *energy and materials management*, since all building activities involve the utilization, redistribution, and concentration of some component of the earth's energy and material resources from usually distant locations into specific areas, changing the ecology of that part of the biosphere as well as adding to the composition of the ecosystem. However, the continued existence and maintenance of this built environment will be dependent on the earth's ecosystem and resources to continue to supply it with certain inputs (e.g., minerals, fuels, air, water, soils, etc.) and processes. In an ecological approach, the designer must be aware of all such external-to-internal exchanges that take place and any environmental interactions (impacts) that result from these exchanges. Holistically, the inputs into the built environment are related to and interdependent with the discharge of outputs, the set of operations in the built environment, and the limitations of the earth's ecosystems and resources.

Pattern of Use and Route

Along the route that each element of the energy or material inputs takes throughout the life cycle of a designed system, a series of interactions with the ecosystems takes place. For instance, the techniques for mining and extraction of mineral supplies cause widespread habitat destruction. Large amounts of energy and other material resources are used, and equally large amounts of waste materials are produced during the processing of these materials and while fabricating and preparing them for use in the built environment. If we conceive the built environment as one segment in the flow of energy and materials through the ecosystem, we can trace this flow and the route taken by each of the inputs. As discussed earlier, the use of energy and materials in the built environment can be regarded as a *pattern of use* in the context of its life cycle. The total set of inputs to the built environment is structured in Fig. 6-1, where the pattern of use consists of the following phases:

- Production
- Construction
- Operation
- Recovery

These in their entirety make up the *external-to-internal* exchanges of the built environment.

Ecological Interactions and Consequences of the External-to-Internal Exchanges of Energy and Materials from the Environment to the Designed System

Many of the consequences of resource use by humans are not readily apparent to the designer,

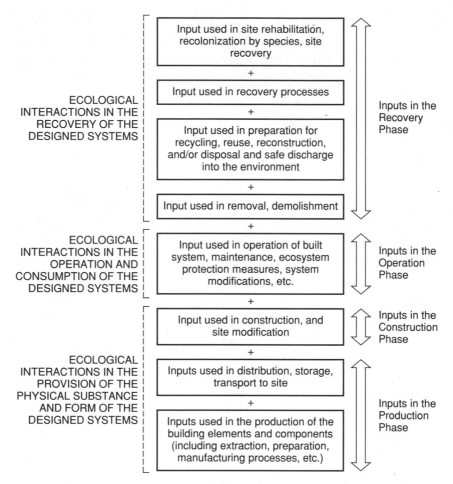

Figure 6-1. The total inputs in the life cycle of a designed system.

who, at present, tends to consider only their assembly phase and their erection on the building site.

The route taken by every resource could be traced, in principle, from its environmental source to its environmental sink. In the process of making the resource available for use in a designed system, considerable impacts on the environment are effected.

For example, the mining and other extraction techniques required for the provision of metals causes habitat destruction. Mineral rocks are removed from the mine, and waste rocks are usually piled somewhere nearby. As demand increases and reserves decrease, lower-grade ores are mined, and the area of land and volume of rock laid waste both rise correspondingly. Large quantities of energy and materials are used to mine, transport, and process materials, and equally large amounts of waste materials and energy are produced. The slag and the gases from the refining process must be disposed of in some way. Finally, when the mine is exhausted, the result is usually a degraded landscape rife with excavated holes, piles of bare rock, and derelict buildings and machinery (LaPorte, 1972). To rehabilitate and revegetate the degraded landscape would require further expenditure of energy and material resources. In addition, the distribution, use, and finally disposal of the built products use up more energy and materials and create more wastes.

Figure 6-2 shows simply the production phase in the life cycle of a single building element. In each of the compartments, however, some ecological interaction takes place. Therefore, each of the processes in each compartment has an impact, to a larger or lesser extent, on the ecosystem in which it takes place, besides at the same time requiring energy and material exchanges as inputs in order to function. In addition, each of the processes requires plants and machinery, building enclosures, and a supply of energy and materials to operate. For instance, the complex set of inputs needed to enable one process (e.g., mining) to take place is shown in Fig. 6-3.

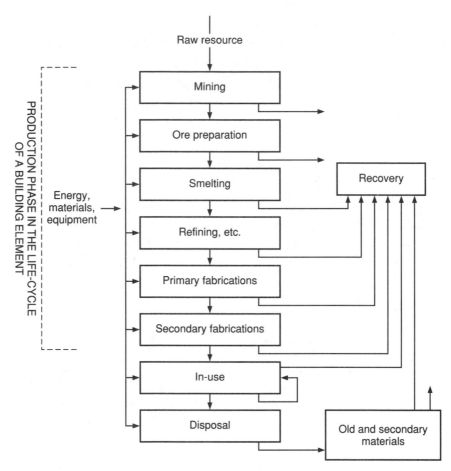

Figure 6-2. Production phase in the life cycle of a single building element (a metal).

The designer needs to be aware of the fact that inherent in the use of each element in a built system is a history of direct and indirect interactions (impacts) with the ecosystems, each including some use of the earth's resources. We can check this with the interactions framework. Each activity in the production of an element for use in a built system will, first, have a spatial and systemic impact on the ecosystems of the geographical location where it

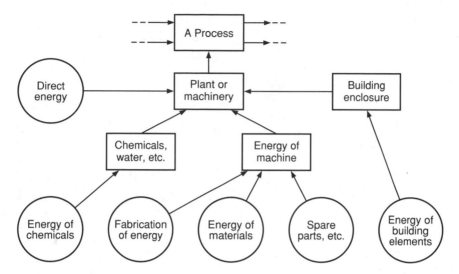

Figure 6-3. The primary inputs to a single process in the built environment.

takes place; second, affect other activities within the built environment; third, consume energy and material inputs in order to operate; and fourth, produce outputs of energy and materials which may interact with the ecosystems and contribute to the environmental contamination problem. *These in toto add up to the ecological consequences of the external-to-internal exchanges of energy and materials from the environment to the built environment.* In order to assess the total ecological consequences, an examination of the following would be necessary:

- The total set of processes and activities involved in making available for use each material resource or energy resource in a designed system
- The spatial and systemic impacts of each of these activities or processes on the ecosystem of the geographical location in which it takes place

- The total set of inputs of energy and materials used in each of these processes and activities, and their respective impacts on the ecosystems
- The total set of outputs of energy and materials emitted in each of these processes and activities, and their respective impacts on the ecosystems.

Furthermore, all these are interrelated and their net impacts constitute the ecological implications of the use of energy and material resources as inputs in a designed system. In a rigorous ecological approach, a comprehensive description of the ecological interaction of the supply of inputs into the built environment is certainly a slavish and complex task. It would entail tracing the ecological consequences of every material and energy resource used in a built structure back to its origin and then continuing through to its reabsorption (when discarded) into the biosphere. To facilitate analysis, *indicators* could be used; an approximation of such an analysis is shown in Fig. 6-4.

The Design Implications for the Conservation of Inputs

A decrease in the use of high ecological-impact materials and forms of energy as a result of the efficient use of alternative materials would only reduce to some extent the overall impact on the biosphere. *The best long-term solution is to reduce the overall demand through the modification of human patterns of needs (i.e., a reduction in the standard of living) and through the general practice of conservation in the use of material and energy resources.*

Items	Energy cost (kWh/kg)	
Metals		
Iron: finished steel	13.2	(Chapman, 1974)
special steel	60.0	(")
Copper	20.0	(")
Zinc	14.7	(")
Lead	12.9	(")
Aluminum	90.0	(")
Titanium	141.2	(")
Electrically processed	51.2	(")
metals (average)		
Tin	—	
Mercury	—	
Magnesium	—	
Gold	—	
Silver	—	
Platinum	—	
Uranium	—	
Beryllium	—	
Radium	—	
Manganese	—	
Nonrenewable fuels		
Petroleum:		
Aviation spirit	11.1 (kWh/L)	(Chapman, 1974)
Motor spirit (3-star)	11.3 (")	(")
Kerosene	12.0 (")	(")
Gas/diesel oil	12.6 (")	(")
Marine diesel oil	12.7 (")	(")
Lubricating oils	12.9 (")	(")
Natural gas	10.1 (kWh/m^3)	(")
Methane	10.3 (")	(")
Coal		
(to power stations)	8.02	(")
(to coke ovens)	9.79	(")
(to iron and steel industry)	9.01	(")

Figure 6-4. Energy cost of production of materials (adapted from Beckman and Weidt, 1973).

Items	Energy cost (kWh/kg)		
Coal			
(domestic)	9.55		(Chapman, 1974)
(railways)	10.28		(")
(other industries)	8.87		(")
Coke	9.22		(")
Pitch	10.00		(")
Other Materials			
Sand and gravel	0.02		(Chapman, 1974)
Stone	—		(")
Cement materials	2.3		(")
Plaster	0.3		(McKillop, 1972)
Lime	1.3		
Sulfur	—		
Salt	—		
Silica	—		
Feldspar	—		
Clay	—		
Asbestos	—		
Fertilizer Materials			
Phosphate (P O)	2.3		(Leach, 1973)
Potash (K O)	2.6		(")
Nitrates	18.9		(")
Other Building Materials			
Brick	0.95	(kWh/kg)	(Chapman, 1974)
Glass	80	(kWh/m^2)	(")
Paper	6.4		(")
Plastics: PVC	19.27		(")
polyethylene	12.19		(")
others (average)	30.00		(")
Synthetic rubber	19.6		(")
Crolite	46.3		(")
Paint	106.6	(kWh/m^2)	(McKillop, 1972)
Water	0.0022	(kWh/L)	(Chapman, 1974)
Timber	70.0	(kWh/m^3)	(McKillop, 1972)

Figure 6-4. (*Continued*)

Looking at the life cycle of a built structure, it is usually in the design stage that many decisions are made that critically affect the amount of energy and materials used. It is the designer who initially specifies the type and qualities of the materials to be used. The processing and fabrication methods chosen for the manufacture and recovery of a product (selected by the designer) determine how much waste will be generated.

The importance of our early design decisions needs to be emphasized. For instance, an unwise choice of materials might lead to a premature failure, necessitating replacement for the element, which would increase the number of products produced and the amount of resources consumed. Moreover, if the faulty product had been designed to be an inseparable part of a larger assembly, then all other materials in that assembly might be wasted (Ballard, 1974). Similarly, in materials processing, the selection of fabrication methods that require excessive machinery and/or excessive waste will increase the total (or gross) amount of materials and energy resources consumed per unit of product.

In contrast, when an efficient design reduces the total amount of resources required per unit, consumption of energy and material resources decreases, and the total flow of energy and materials through the built environment is decreased. Design should ensure that the processes chosen for the built environment use the least mass and the least energy of the alternatives available to perform a desired service. This means that the designer has to do more with fewer resources (Fuller, 1963). A rational use of energy and material resources means a design approach that is based on resource conservation principles.

Such a design approach based on conservation of resources can be considered in terms of the following alternative design strategies: *(1) measures that reduce the supply to the system, (2) measures that improve the efficiency and performance of existing systems, and (3) general measures for the redesign of existing systems or the design of new systems.* These strategies are elaborated below.

1. *Measures that reduce the supply and flow rate are those which*
   - Reduce the existing consumption level by controlling the rate of resource use or lowering the standard of living
   - Reduce flow by reducing the total number of products turned out
   - Substitute the use of other resources (e.g., renewable resources)

2. *Measures that improve the efficiency and performance of existing systems are those which*
   - Encourage the recovery (reuse, recycling, and regeneration) of existing products, provided it does not increase environmental degradation and contamination
   - Increase the efficiency of recovery processes
   - Extend the useful life of a unit of a product
   - Control corrosion and wear losses
   - Increase the efficiency of production processes
   - Increase the efficiency of product use

3. *General design measures for the redesign of existing systems or the design of new systems include*

- Achievement of materials and energy economy and low ecological impact by appropriate design and selection
- Redesign of existing systems toward maximum performance
- Design for ease of repair and recovery, e.g., by standardization and simplification of materials and products
- Design for optimum use life of a unit of product
- Design for minimum use of materials per unit of product
- Design for efficiency and low ecological impact in processing and recovery
- Design for efficiency and low ecological impact in use

The above measures are of course not exhaustive of all the methods of designing for resource conservation, but are indicative of the ways in which our design efforts might be directed.

Energy Indices as Indicators of Environmental Impact

Energy is a critical variable in the built environment. The present exploitation of material resources is heavily dependent on fossil fuels as sources of energy. The availability of nonrenewable resources also tends constantly downward, and in most cases, can be recovered only at the expense of added energy expenditure, which has to come from somewhere.

It is generally true that all existing major building developments are fossil-fuel-dependent and have been designed to be fuel extravagant. However, the built environment was seldom seen in its entirety from an energy viewpoint until recently (e.g., Yeang, 1974b). For instance, considerable energy is consumed in the creation of a building and in maintaining it. Energy is consumed in the building operation, in moving people and goods to and from it, and in tearing it down. The built system also has major effects on the energy flows of its surroundings and on the people who use it. Furthermore, measures to cope with its attendant environmental problems also require expenditure of energy, e.g., the recycling of solid wastes and curtailing of air pollution. In general, buildings and their related facilities account for about 30 to 40 percent of the energy consumed by the man-made environment annually, and transportation further consumes another 25 percent of the total (Bender, 1973). Simply increasing the availability of the energy supply will only result in the augmentation of existing flow rates and the concentration of materials. This would also only exacerbate the problems by reinforcing the existing patterns of use. The availability of energy resources (nonrenewable) is also a key factor in the availability of the other material resources, and subsequently in the functioning of the built environment. The use of fossil fuels further adds to the earth's environmental burden. Our design efforts should therefore obviously be directed toward an overall reduction in consumption.

A general indicator of any designed system's value (or an essential service's total cost) is the net result of an accounting that adds up the quantities of the energy (nonrenewable) which went into its making (e.g., Berdurski, 1973). For instance, it can be seen that certain products consume more energy per unit than others (Hammon, 1973).

The energy cost of a designed system can be further seen in the context of its life cycle. For instance, the amount of fuel required to operate a building during its useful lifetime is large (around 65 percent) compared with the total energy invested in its production and construction. It has been found that for every kilowatthour of energy consumed in the construction of large office buildings (including energy used in the manufacture of materials, transportation, etc.), approximately one kWh of energy will be used per year in its life cycle to operate the building services (GSA, 1974).

If we take into account the facts that all resource use has an inevitable impact on the ecological environment, and that the quantities of energy resources used in the existing man-made environment have been derived from mainly nonrenewable sources, then the inputs of the built environment can be accounted for in design using a form of "energy equivalents" (e.g., Makhijani and Lichtenberg, 1972; Hirst, 1973; Chapman, 1973, 1974) as indicators of impacts (see Fig. 6-4).

In ecology, *energetics* is defined as the study of the ecosystem in terms of energy exchanges and metabolism (or efficiencies), where the biomass of an ecosystem is converted into energy and units. In a similar way, the energy flows through a built system, and the energy stock of the built system can be commensurately quantified using energy indices, e.g., the energy cost of producing common building materials (Beckman and Weidt, 1973; Chapman, 1973; Yeang, 1974a, b). As an index, the energy cost of a product gives a crude measure of the product's impact on the use of energy resources. It is indicative of the complexity of its production in comparison to other products. It can also be used in assessing current technology by totaling all the energy used in the product's production, operation, and disposal or recovery. In a similar way, the energy cost of different forms of construction could be compared (e.g., Brown and Stetlon, 1974) as a broad indicator of their dependency on the earth's energy resources.

In summary, the external-to-internal exchanges from its environment to a designed system consist of those inputs of energy and materials that are directed from the environment into the designed system for its realization and operation (including its maintenance and disposal processes). Some of the considerations affecting design are as follows:

1. In a rigorous ecological approach to design, a thorough analysis and quantification of the inputs of the energy and material resources that are used in the life cycle, as well as an inventory of their respective impairment of the ecosystem would be necessary (Patterson, 1990; Roaf and Hancock, 1992).

2. In addition to the functional criteria for the selection of materials and energy forms for use in building, design criteria should include the environmental impact of that use of the energy or material throughout the designed system's life cycle as well as its status as a resource (whether renewable or nonrenewable). The task is a complex one because each process in the built environment uses resources and has its own set of impacts on the environment.

3. The purposes of considering these inputs to the built environment as part of the design considerations are threefold:

   - To reduce the depletion of the biosphere's resource base
   - To reduce the outputs generated by the built environment into the ecological environment
   - To reduce the use of the ecosystems as a result of the use of these inputs

4. The analysis of these exchanges to the built environment in relation to their ecosystem interactions and impacts would provide the designer with a basis for

   - Comparing the total consequences in terms of the use of materials and energy of one design against those of another design. This would facilitate the choice of subsystems in design.
   - The conservation of nonrenewable energy and material resources by designing and planning for efficient use and minimum consumption.
   - Reducing the direct and the indirect influences of the inputs of the built environment on the ecosystems by a reduction in consumption and the total throughput of the built environment.
   - Determining which aspects of the built environment consume excessive resources, and which aspects could subsequently be modified or redesigned to achieve a more efficient use.
   - Determining the use of inputs in the context of a life cycle so that resources could be relocated from areas of wasteful or unnecessary consumption to other areas of use (e.g., for recycling or recovery).

5. Design strategies for resource conservation include measures that reduce the supply and the flow rate, measures that improve the efficiency and performance of existing systems, and general measures for the redesign of existing systems or the design of new systems.

6. To facilitate consideration, energy indices may be used as simple indicators of environmental impacts.

In this chapter, we have examined the ecological implications of the use of energy and material resources in the built environment. In the ecological design approach, we should ensure that our built systems and processes use the least amount of materials and the least energy of the alternatives available to perform a desired function or service. This would require the designer to choose a design that requires fewer resources. A rational use of energy and material resource means a design approach that is based on resource conservation principles.

7
Internal-to-External Ecological Interdependencies of the Built Environment

The Emissions from the Built Environment into the Environment

The internal-to-external exchanges of the built environment are those internal-to-external dependencies of the built environment which consist of the internal-to-external exchanges of energy and materials from the built environment to the ecosystems in the form of outputs or waste products (Wann, 1990). These are the exchanges of energy and materials which are discharged from the built environment into the ecosystems to be either assimilated or

161

absorbed into the ecosystems (with or without some form of pretreatment). These exchanges represent the internal-to-external "transactional interdependencies" of the built environment.

The management of such outputs has been commonly categorized in related disciplines dealing with environmental protection, such as *pollution control, solid-waste disposal, air-pollution engineering, water-pollution engineering, and liquid-effluents disposal* (e.g., Hammon, 1973). Many if not most of these are largely piecemeal approaches, and they are clearly inadequate because they usually consider only one environmental medium (e.g., air or water) to the exclusion of others. Nevertheless, it is generally acknowledged that such exchanges take place in the environment and that some form of corrective measure is needed, especially in cases where ecosystem contamination poses a problem.

The discharge and management of outputs are related systemically to and interdependent with the flow of inputs, the operations within the built environment, and the assimilative capacity of the earth's ecosystems. In the design process, it is necessary for the designer to anticipate the net outputs associated with the proposed designed system (i.e., the outputs discharged in its life cycle), the impacts and interactions that these may have with the ecosystems, the extent and type of inputs used in managing these outputs, and the ways they can be managed cyclically within the built environment. We can represent the total outputs of a designed system in relation to its life cycle as in Fig. 7-1.

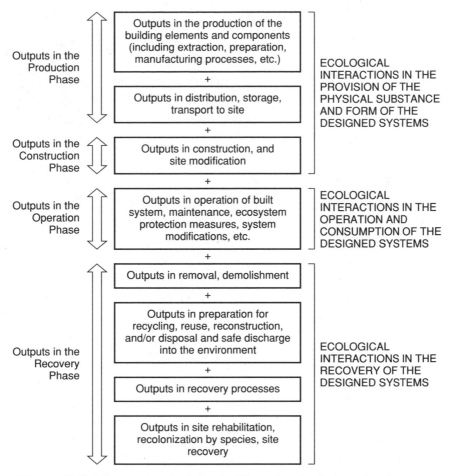

Figure 7-1. The total outputs in the life cycle of a designed system.

The Generation of Waste from the Built Environment

As we have stated earlier, the generation of outputs and their introduction into the environment is characteristic of all open systems (Bolittho, 1973).

Generally, waste disposal is an inevitable activity in all human societies, even those with purely agricultural economies. For example, when land is plowed, there is inevitably some runoff of organic materials. The simplest cooking fire releases smoke and carbon dioxide into the atmosphere. Human life, like any life, leaves organic wastes. However, what is different in all of these is the manner in which the outputs are managed.

The existing built environment generates outputs throughout all phases of its life cycle. For example, in many production processes in the built environment, the material outputs make up 25 to 50 percent by weight of the outputs (Bower, 1971). Outputs from construction processes include the rubble of the structure, concrete, bricks, timber cutoffs, metalwork, etc. Solid outputs from domestic buildings during their period of use consist mainly of paper and fermentable organic matter with frequent dust, cinders, textiles, glass, porcelain, wood, metals, and plastics. Outputs from commercial buildings during their period of use are largely paper-based, but include food wastes. Industrial outputs include building wastes, plastic, wood, textiles, ash, gaseous emissions, liquid effluents from production processes, and other toxic discharges. As the activities of the man-made environment increase in amount and diversity, so will the forms of the output.

Generally, no matter how well our built environment has been designed and operated, there will inevitably be end products that need to be disposed of. However, the designer cannot expect these unwanted outputs to disappear, nor can he or she expect to throw them away elsewhere. Although the designer may be able to reduce, change, or convert the form of any output, what finally remains has to be eventually disposed of into the ecosystems. Although some outputs may be kept in use cyclically within the built environment by means of recovery processes, it should be remembered that the final sinks for any unwanted output are the ecosystems in the biosphere.

The importance of retaining the viability of the earth's ecosystems is again emphasized. Theoretically, any living system can remain stable only if the larger environment of which it is a differentiated part is capable of absorbing its outputs at the rate at which they are produced. When the discharge of the outputs of the system is not controlled, it will steadily reduce the order of the larger environment by replacing its highly differentiated parts with waste or random parts. By degrading its own environment in this way, the system that is emitting the outputs is creating its own death or failure, as it cannot survive in an environment made up of random parts, i.e., displaying total entropy. The analogy of the survival of the organism with its environment is clear. *The organism that destroys its environment destroys itself.* Each system must endeavor to eliminate all unfavorable outputs because failure to do so will result in the need to create secondary systems to solve problems of disposal, which will incur a further environmental cost. The closed-resource concept of the biosphere illuminates the tradeoffs that are involved in having more of one system's products at the expense of the other's. Unless the problem of disposal is considered, the outputs remain a liability, and the existing condition of the environment will deteriorate further. The management of outputs that are emitted from a proposed design must therefore be considered at the outset as part of the design process.

Identification and Inventory of Outputs

Before we can decide on the form of output management, we need to identify and inventory all the exchanges from our designed system. The designer can view the outputs from the built environment in many ways. For example, they can be classified according to their *physical form* (solid, liquid, gaseous, particulate) or their *type* and *toxicity* (SO_2, hydrocarbons, mercury compounds, etc.).

Alternatively, the outputs from the built environment can be viewed in relation to their *source of generation*. For instance, outputs from the built environment consist of the following:

- The by-products, residual substances or leftovers from the construction of the built environment, e.g., timber cutoffs, main tailings, rejects, etc. These are collectible, and, if technically possible, they should be either recycled or received; otherwise their assimilation and disposal into the environment will need to be considered.

- The unavoidable losses from the operation of the designed system (e.g., friction losses, thermal losses from processes, transmission losses, etc.). These are given a separate category because they are not physically recoverable, although they can be minimized if the technical means are available.

- The designed system itself at the end of its useful life, when its disposal will have to be dealt with (e.g., building materials, materials from demolition activities, packaging, etc.). Unless a lower form of reuse is possible, these are collectible and can be recycled, reused, or recovered.
- Other outputs associated with the activity or process, e.g., the creation of dust by production or handling processes.

In a rigorous ecological approach, the route that each output takes within the environment in all the phases of the cycle of activities in the designed system should be examined so as to ensure that the outputs do not cause environmental impairment, whether singularly or synergistically.

This categorization of outputs further shows the lack of comprehensiveness of many of the existing methods of pollution control and planning currently in use. Much environmental contamination may be attributed to the fact that the substance that caused the pollution has not previously been considered as a possible pollution problem.

We can further consider outputs as a limiting factor in design. In cases where the outputs need to be assimilated into the ecosystems, this distinction can facilitate their consideration. A fundamental distinction between two basic types of outputs can be made (Odum, E. P., 1971, p. 75):

- Those that involve an increase in the volume or rate of introduction of material and/or energy already present in the ecosystems
- Those that involve poisons and chemicals that are not normally present in the ecosystems

The Management of the Internal-to-External Exchanges from the Built Environment

As we have mentioned earlier, to design a built environment as a completely closed system without any exchanges of energy and materials with its external environment is not possible in practice, since external environmental interactions are necessary attributes of living systems. Accepting the premise that some environmental interactions and exchanges are inevitable, design must initially aim at reducing that generation of outputs in the first instance, since the outputs, once produced, cannot be easily managed without expending additional energy and/or material resources and incurring further environmental burdens. We can conclude that an important design task is the reduction and anticipation of output generation in our early design stages, as the above limitations exist once the output is produced. We can define output management here as *the decisions that have to be made by the designer regarding the pathways taken by the outputs, the form in which they go through, their terminal destination, and the interactions with the impacts on the ecosystems along the route.* These are fundamental decisions that the designer must be aware of and must make in the preliminary stages of design. They should ideally be the basis behind all output control methods, particularly when dealing with outputs that are highly pollutive.

Generally, we need to endeavor to eliminate by design all unfavorable discharges of outputs from each designed system because our failure to do so will result in the need to create further secondary systems to solve subsequent problems of disposal, which will incur further environmental burdens. The management of outputs must therefore be considered at the outset as part of our design process (see Figs. 7-2 and 7-3).

Outputs	Examples of existing treatment process
Airborne	
Particulates	Settling chamber
Hydrocarbons	Cyclone
Sulfur oxides	Electrostatic precipitation
Carbon monoxides	Fabric filter
Nitrogen oxides	Wet scrubber
Others	Afterburner
Waterborne	
Biochemical oxygen demand	Screening
Suspended solids	Sedimentation
Dissolved solids	Equalization and storage
Total phosphate	Chemical addition
Total nitrogen	Activated filter
Heat	Trickling filter
Heavy metal	Ion exchange
Others	
Land-borne	
Solid waste:	Incineration
Paper and paper products	Open dumping
Garbage and other	Sanitary infill
organic materials	Recovery: reuse, recycle,
Demolition materials	reconstitute
Other incombustibles	
(cans, bottles, etc.)	
Debris from dispersed sources	
(street scrapings, materials	
conveyed in storm runoffs)	
Abandoned vehicles	

Figure 7-2. Outputs from the built environment and examples of ways of treating them.

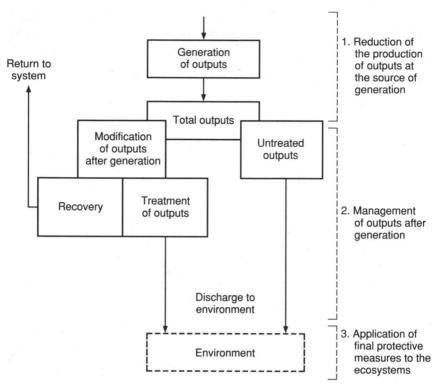

Figure 7-3. Map of the possible routes taken by the outputs from the built environment. This is a generic model for tracing the flow of outputs from the built environment; it could be considered as a problem definition tool. No equivalent status is accorded to each of the measures listed. The selection of the appropriate form of management for each individual output from a system will thus depend on the built system, the form of outputs discharged, the operating conditions, the form of the inputs, the state of the environment, and the interaction of all these factors.

Having established in the design process that some form of corrective measure is needed, the designer must then determine the possible design strategy. The designer should consider the problem as a whole, checking against the interactions framework. The prevalent use of quick *technological fixes* by most pollution engineers discourages the consideration of other alternatives. For instance, if water pollution threatens, the current tendency is to use technical solutions to treat the emissions (e.g., diluting the water or treating the wastes) instead of considering ways to prevent the emissions. *In a rigorous ecological approach to design, the designer should monitor every emission and its influence on the ecosystems.* In practice, this is not achievable in absolute terms. Nevertheless, before the form of output management can be determined, the nature of the outputs that are discharged must be firmly established and any destructive influences anticipated. In order that the effects and importance of the disturbance can be assessed, answers to the following questions should be sought by the designer at the outset, as he or she determines the life cycle of the proposed design:

1. What is being discharged? (Consider the type, form, source, and volume of outputs.)
2. Where does it have its effects? (Consider the emission sources, the spatial location, and the range of its impacts.)
3. What effect does it have? (Consider the assessment of the type of damage, its persistence, and the complexity of the outputs.)
4. Does this matter? (Consider the importance of the damage, the assimilative capacity of the environment, and its ability to recover.)
5. Can it be corrected? (Consider the range of possible solutions and design measures and estimate their effectiveness.)
6. Is it being corrected? (Consider enforcement and/or implementation of measures and assessment of their results.)

Ideally, designers should regard the management of outputs as something to be handled *internally* within the built environment and allow emissions only if outputs are not usable internally and/or can be assimilated into the ecological environment without contamination and with low energy and material costs.

Referring to our interactions framework (Chap. 3), our design principle should be one in which there is a tradeoff of these three objectives: *minimum import and minimum export of net energy and material demands, minimum generation and discharge of net outputs, and minimum contamination of the ecosystems.*

The management of outputs usually requires additional expenditures of energy and materials and some added environmental cost. Therefore, in the design and planning of the built environment the designer should ensure that difficult outputs are minimized or are not permitted to be generated in the first place.

Notes on Design Strategies to Correct the Discharge of Outputs

Design measures for output management can be conceived in the following ways: (1) as a reduction of outputs at the source of generation, (2) as the management of outputs after generation, and (3) as the application of final protective measures. These measures may be related to the pathways taken by the outputs, as shown in Fig. 7-4.

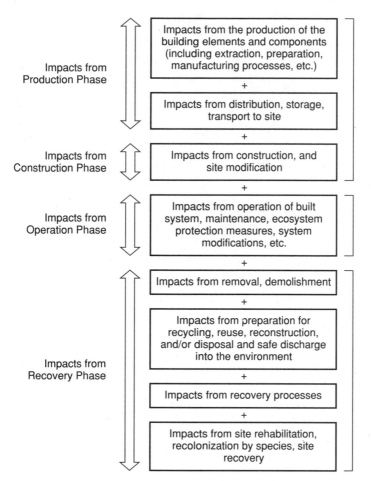

Figure 7-4. Impacts in the life cycle of a designed system.

1. *The reduction of outputs at the source of generation.* The designer can either arrange the methods for handling the outputs after they have been generated to suit the design, or else arrange the design to suit the methods of management. The first stage in the management of outputs is to approach the problem at the source of the generation, reducing the generation of outputs and changing their nature and

composition. This measure entails the design modification of the built environment and its production processes, both quantitatively and qualitatively. Physical attributes that would achieve the management goals could be introduced or designed into the system. For example, the enclosure of a short-life building could be designed to facilitate reuse, recycling, regeneration, or biodegradation. Many of these changes can be effected by preliminary design decisions. Some of the methods for the reduction in output generation can be achieved by some combination of the following changes:

- Changing the nature of the inputs (or input mix). For instance, the inputs to any process can be selected in such a way that the product is tailored to its pattern of use or life span. With existing processes, substitute inputs could be used.

- Changing the nature of the outputs or the final product of any process through a change in the product specification (e.g., changing the requirements in the design program).

- Reducing the levels of consumption by the users of the built environment and/or lowering the levels of production of a particular product.

- Changing the nature of the processes which produce the output (e.g., changing the production, construction, consumption, and recovery processes entirely). This would include increasing the efficiency of the processes so as to reduce the production of residuals. The use of energy and material in the built environment can be improved so as to reduce the generation of waste and destructive outputs into the environment.

- Increasing the durability and/or nondurability of the built systems to conform to their pattern of use or life span.
- Scheduling processes in such a way that the mix of outputs, magnitude of emissions, and time and pattern of generation are tailored to the assimilative ability of the environment.

2. *The management of outputs after generation.* Once outputs have been generated in an activity, they can be modified either before discharge into the environment or after they have been discharged directly into the environment. The following is a discussion of the methods of management of outputs after their generation.

- *Recovery of outputs.* In some cases, the useful life of an output can be extended by recovery. Recovery (as a general term) may be described as making one unit of material (and/or energy) serve more than one purpose. The recovery process reduces the overall throughput of the production–consumption system by introducing the recovery component into the cycle of activities. By reducing the throughput, fewer demands are placed on the assimilative ability of the environment. However, there is a threshold to recovery activity, as every act of recovery involves expenditure of energy and materials and some environmental influences on ecosystems. Another reason for recovery might be to reduce the treatment. The feasibility of the recovery of any output depends on the technical means for the activity, the product output specification (or the design program), and the availability of a potential use (or demand) for the recovered output.

The types of recovery are:

Reuse. This involves the reuse of the output in the form in which it is discharged or in a modified form which does not require any additional reprocessing.

Recycling. This involves the use of output after it has undergone some reprocessing, accompanied by a complete or partial change in form without requiring any additional reprocessing.

Regeneration. This involves the partial or total reconstitution of the output into its original form prior to use.

Methods leading to the release and use of energy. To facilitate the recovery of the outputs from the built environment and their cycle of activities, the total pattern of use has to be reviewed. It could be stated that our entire man-made environment needs to be restructured so that it can become more efficient in its use of energy and material resources by recovering the bulk of the resources that are within the man-made environment. It is generally held that a human life-support system based on a recovery pattern of use is the only structure that could operate for an indefinite period of time in a finite system.

■ *Pretreatment of outputs.*   Where the recovery of the output cannot be effected, and where its direct discharge into the environment would result in ecosystem contamination or degradation, some form of pretreatment before its discharge must be considered.

Pretreatment measures involve the neutralization or modification of the output after generation in such a manner that it imposes a lower effective demand on the assimilative ability of the ecosystems in the biosphere. These measures usually take the form of physical, chemical, or biological methods of pretreatment (Tebbutt, 1971, p. 79).

Physical processes are those which depend simply on the physical properties of the output, e.g., particle size, specific gravity, viscosity, etc.

Chemical processes are those which depend on the chemical properties of the output or utilize the chemical properties of added reagents. The choice of a reagent in chemical treatment is important, as the resolution of one problem may result in a far worse one.

Biological processes are those which use the biological properties or biochemical reactions of the output to remove soluble or colloidal organic impurities. Examples are biological filtration and the activated-sludge process.

In most cases, additional expenditures of energy and materials are necessary to carry out the pretreatment processes, and this may create other environmental disturbances elsewhere. The goal of pretreatment is for the form and/or composition of the output to be converted in such a way that it can return to the ecosystems without constriction or impairment. The process should ideally be tailored to function well below the limits of the assimilative ability of the receiving environmental sink. Pretreatment does not reduce the total weight of the outputs, rather it modifies their form and/or the time and space they require. Accompanying the processes must be a nonpolluting method of disposal, a minimization of the inputs needed in the processes, and an understanding of the ecosystems which receive the final output.

- *Detention.*   Certain outputs may be stored temporarily until an advantageous time (NAS-NRC, 1966). One example of the use of such a method is the retention of outputs in a storage system so that their discharge may be scheduled to conform more closely with the rate of assimilation of the receiving environmental sink. Storage hoppers and tanks are sometimes used to segregate one output from another until they are ready for processing (Bolittho, 1973; Chappel, 1973).

In some cases, outputs are concentrated to reduce their volume and then stored until future solutions (for their removal, treatment, recovery, or safe environmental discharge) have been devised. To permit storage, sites would have to be allocated.

This method for dealing with outputs is an incomplete one. Generally, it has been used with toxic and hazardous wastes (e.g., radioactive wastes).

Methods of detention on and off site include, for example:

Containers, bags
Unconfined storage
Controlled atmosphere
Transfer stations
Process centers
On-site post process
Compaction
Refrigeration

- *Dispersion.* This method involves the distribution of an output spatially over a large area of the environment (i.e., air, land, or water) so that the concentration of the output is never sufficient to cause an acute disturbance to the ecosystems (Koenig et al., 1971). An example of such a method can be seen in the case of industrial gaseous discharges, where the use of a higher chimney disperses the emissions over a larger environmental receiving area.

  Alternatively, the activities can be located in a dispersed pattern so that the total emissions are not concentrated in the environmental receiving media. A polluting source can be located so that the targets that need to be shielded are not exposed (Bower et al., 1968; Holgate, 1972).

  Dispersion could be combined with regulation of the time pattern of generation and/or discharge of outputs (e.g., batch discharge or continuous discharge).

- *Dilution.* In this method, the output is diluted with a medium in such a way as to augment its volume and the assimilative ability of the environmental receiving sink.

- *Diversion.* Where outputs are generated in locations which are unsuitable for discharge, the outputs can be transported or diverted to another location that has more favorable assimilative ability or that is less contaminated. As suitable locations are exhausted, the use of this method will be limited. Transportation and diversion would incur further expenditures of energy and material resources as inputs.

3. *The application of final protective measures.* In a case where certain components of the ecosystems are of particular importance to the designer, the application of final protective measures between the ambient conditions and the ecosystem's components (e.g., humans, animals, plants, and inanimate objects) can be carried out. These can take the following forms:

- *Environmental treatment.* Instead of treating outputs at their source, the environmental receiving sink is treated in order to diminish the effects of the outputs. One use of this method could be to prevent the synergistic effects of a number of outputs. As pointed out earlier, this method should be carried out only when its effects are predictable and when it would not lead to other induced effects on the ecological environment. Additional expenditures of energy and materials are obviously needed. Generally, the method provides short-term partial effectiveness in the control of pollution. Its main uses are for cases of accidental discharges, e.g., oil spills. The receiving environment can in some cases be modified to improve its assimilation capacity. At present, the alternatives are few. Examples are in water-quality management, stream aeration, and low-flow augmentation (Spofford, 1971).

- *Environmental desensitization.* In this method, the environmental receiving medium and sink are desensitized so that the impact of the contaminants is not apparent or felt. For example, scent can be sprayed onto polluted beaches to reduce the odors. Included in this approach are measures that protect the receptors (e.g., humans, flora, and fauna) from an already degraded environment. The output and receptors could be separated by a spatial zone. Depending on the scale of the operation, energy and material inputs are required. The method should be used in situations where the contamination has reached such a point that no other measures can be used.

Identification of the Time, Location, and Pattern of Discharge

All the outputs that are finally discharged into the environment make use of the biosphere as a receiving sink and of the biosphere's ability to assimilate the outputs. The biological and physical constituents of the ecosystems within the biosphere are thus the final receiving sink for the outputs. The receiving sink can be considered spatially as consisting of the atmospheric environment, the aquatic and marine environments, and the terrestrial environment.

The ecosystems have the capacity to assimilate, to some degree, most forms and types of residuals through the natural ecosystem mechanisms of transport, transformation, and storage. The use of the ecosystem as a receiving sink for the outputs could be described as the use of the systems' assimilative ability (i.e., their ability to dissipate, absorb, dilute, degrade, decompose, or modify the outputs).

Ecological imbalance occurs when a discharge results in a significant impairment of some of the components or propensities in the ecosystems, in which case the outputs are termed pollutants.

Within this frame of reference, *pollution can be defined as the introduction into or the presence within the ecosystems of materials or forms of energy, derived from human activities, in quantities and forms which have destructive and unwanted effects on the ecosystems*. Usually, these are substances that do not occur naturally in the ecosystems or that occur in different quantities or in a different ratio from what is normally present in the ecosystem (Ashby, 1971).

The capacity of the ecosystem to assimilate outputs varies from place to place and from time to time, depending upon local conditions, upon the stochastic nature of some of the variables of the ecosystem (e.g., stream flow, temperature, sunlight, etc.), and upon the nature of the discharge of outputs.

In the majority of cases, a network of cause–condition–effects appears when the outputs discharged into the ecological environment exceed the limits of the ecosystems to assimilate them. As pointed out earlier, excessive damage in one part of the biosphere may affect the functioning of another part. The pollution of an ecosystem in one locality can be transported by an environmental medium to another locality, and this may modify the quality and supply of resources from that location.

For an ecosystem that has been upset by an output, a new equilibrium must be found. When the pollution is not severe, the system may restabilize, and if the pollution is halted, the system may achieve a new equilibrium in time. When the emission of the output continues unabated and exceeds what the components of the ecosystem can tolerate, severe impairment of the ecosystem's processes, structure, and properties will result, culminating in the disorganization and destruction of the ecosystem or its continuation in a state in which only organisms that are able to exist in the impaired conditions will be able to flourish.

To a certain extent, as long as destructive impacts are not effected and the ecosystem balance is maintained, the ecosystem's assimilative properties can be used for the discharge of outputs. Since not all outputs can be kept in use within the built environment without excessive expenditures of energy and materials, the majority of effluents may have to be discharged into the ecological environment.

To determine the assimilative capacity of the receiving environment, the biological and physical constraints of the ecosystem and the nature and discharge patterns of the outputs must be known.

From the design point of view, it is necessary to be able to translate a specified time, location, and pattern of discharges of outputs into the resulting time and areal pattern of the ambient environmental conditions. In most cases, there are multiple sources of discharge, which complicate the conditions.

There is usually a tradeoff of the factors involved. To take one extreme, a built-up region that concentrated heavily on electric space heating, electric transportation systems, and wet scrubbing of stack gases (from steam plants and industries) and that ground up its garbage and delivered it to the sewers and then discharged the untreated sewage to the watercourses would protect its atmospheric environment to an exceptional degree. But this would come at the expense of placing a heavy output load upon the aquatic environment. On the other hand, a region that treated its municipal and industrial wastewater streams to a high level and relied heavily on the incineration of sludges and solid wastes would protect its aquatic and terrestrial environment at the expense of the aerial environment. Finally, a region that practiced high-level recovery and recycling of waste materials and fostered low residual production processes to a far-reaching extent in each sector of the man-made environment might discharge very little residual output into any of the environmental media but would use excessive input of energy and materials to enable the recovery processes to take place. In all instances, the use of our interactions framework in the analysis of the pollution problem would assist in identifying those aspects that need to be taken into consideration.

To anticipate the ecosystem impacts of each output, consider that after their discharge into the ecosystems, the outputs can ecologically undergo only three basic mechanisms or processes within and/or between ecosystems (Bower and Spofford, 1970):

- Transport (i.e., within the ecosystems by means of an environmental medium)
- Transformation or modification (i.e., physical, chemical, or biological conversion from one mix of output characteristics to another)
- Storage or accumulation (i.e., its state in the atmosphere, in watercourses and sea, on the land, and in biological systems)

Generally, in our ecological approach, the routes that the outputs take in the ecosystems and their impacts on the ecological environment must be anticipated before their discharge. For instance, even a 1°C increase in the annual surface temperature of an aquatic ecosystem as a result of thermal emissions could cause changes in the boundaries between biotic communities (Waggoner, 1966).

In summary, the internal-to-external exchanges of energy and materials from the built environment to the ecosystems are its outputs or waste products, the energy and materials that are discharged from the built environment into the ecosystems to be assimilated or absorbed into the ecosystems, whether with or without some form of pretreatment. These represent the internal-to-external transactional interdependencies of the built environment.

The management of the outputs from our built environment corresponds to disciplines that deal with the handling and disposal of wastes (e.g., refuse disposal, recycling technology, pollution control, etc.). All these, however, need to be reviewed using our interactions framework.

The total outputs from a designed system are the outputs emitted throughout its life cycle, that is, from its production phase through construction and operation to the recovery phase. The management of these needs to be evaluated and traded off in relation to the net inputs of energy and materials with which they are carried out and the effects of any discharged residues on the ecosystem.

The designer has to ensure that the outputs that are discharged during the life cycle of a built system are inventoried, monitored, their routes traced, and their effects on the ecosystems evaluated and minimized. Answers to the following questions must be sought early in the design process:

- What is being discharged? (type, form, source, and volume of outputs)
- Where does it have its effects? (emission sources, the spatial location, and the range of its impacts)
- What effects does it have? (assessment of the type of damage, its persistence, and the complexity of the outputs)
- Does this matter? (the importance of the damage, the assimilative capacity of the environment, and its ability to recover)
- Can it be corrected? (the range of possible solutions and the design measures and an estimate of their effectiveness)
- Is it being corrected? (enforcement and/or implementation of measures and assessment of their results)

Design measures for the management of outputs can be conceived in the following ways:

- A reduction of the production of outputs at the source of generation
- The management of outputs after generation
- The application of final protection measures

8
Ecological Design

Environmental problems can be broadly defined as the changes in ecosystem conditions that arise from the stresses caused by a human action or activity. These involve one or all of these three impacts: depletion of and/or alteration of and/or addition to the earth's ecosystems and resources. Based on these impacts, an ecological architecture would be one that minimizes the changes that have adverse impacts on the earth's ecology (i.e., depletion, alteration, or addition).

Ecological design is a design process in which the designer comprehensively minimizes the anticipated adverse effects that the product of that design process has upon the earth's ecosystems and resources, and simultaneously gives priority to the continued elimination and minimization of these adverse effects.

To achieve this goal, it is evident that an interdisciplinary approach to ecological design that embodies ecology and architecture and other related disciplines (concerned with the problems of the protection, conservation, and preservation of the environment) is needed.

Unfortunately, most architects and designers do not have adequate knowledge of ecology and environ-

187

mental biology; besides, at present, there is no *central unifying theory* or commonly acceptable concept defining what ecological architecture is. The immediate objective, therefore, is to develop a unifying theoretical basis and frame of reference for design, without which any effort at ecological design would remain piecemeal or linear. In this regard, our interactions framework provides a holistic theory for design.

Architecture is more than the art of decorative building; it is also a social art and a considerable number of disciplines claim a stake in defining its body of knowledge. Ecology now has a right to this claim. Ecology, being a natural science, is concerned with the survival of humans as a biotic component in the biosphere, which they are constantly modifying. Their architecture and urban development contribute substantially to this ongoing process of environmental modification and impairment. If designers were able to approach design with a better understanding of the relationship and conflicts between architecture and ecology, the result would likely be a reduction of the present state of environmental impairment.

Our existing theoretical bases of architecture must therefore be expanded to include the ecological implications of construction, use, and disposal. While the need for ecological design has been generally recognized as vital in recent years (e.g., Commoner, 1971; Moorcraft, 1972), a connection between architecture and ecology must become inherent in the building practice.

Architectural research at present might be regarded as being centered around either the *spatial* (e.g., Martin, 1966) or the *climatic* model (Hillier, 1977). The ecological approach to design, however, encompasses both these models. For instance, any built form spatially displaces the ecosystem upon which it is located by virtue of its physical presence and form. Besides this areal impact, the built form also modifies the climate, which itself is one of the major determining factors of an ecosystem. The built environment as a system and the earth with its ecosystems as the environment must both be considered simultaneously in the ecological approach to design.

A further area of architectural research is the study of the ecosystemic interactions of architecture with its environment. In the ecological approach, the designer must be concerned not only with the designed system's spatial impacts on and interactions with the ecosystems of the project site, but also systemically with the interactions of the types and quantities of energy and materials used in the designed system's physical fabric and form, its internal processes and the way their outputs are discharged into the environment, and the ecosystem's response to these interactions.

Our framework here provides the designer with a comprehensive and holistic theory for ecological design. It is clear that each of its four components corresponds with one of the sets of demands that any built environment makes on the earth's ecosystems. Each is connected to the other disciplines concerned with environmental pollution, protection, and conservation. Therefore, the framework provides us with a fundamental basis from which ecological design and all other problems of environmental impairment should be approached.

Architectural education must be altered to include ecology and environmental biology as disciplines to

be taught at schools of architecture. In addition to
this, related disciplines, such as resource conservation, inputs control, recycling, energy and materials
management (internalization), and pollution control
(outputs control) are pertinent and must also be
taught.

The traditional view of architecture will have to be
revised in an ecological approach to design. The
ecologist is concerned more specifically with the systemic aspects of architecture than with its aesthetic
or social aspects (even though these aspects may
indirectly have ecological implications in the sense
that they affect the behavior of people in the ecosystem). The ecologist is more concerned with the ecological implications of the built environment's use of
energy and materials and their flow. For the ecologist, the creation of architecture is no more than the
management of energy and material resources
assembled and concentrated in a transient stage in
the context of the processes in the biosphere.
Ecologically, the built environment may be said to be
a potential waste product whose reuse requires further design effort. A work of design may be regarded as more than just a traditional statement of the
designer's aesthetic aspirations and user functions; it
is a physical and symbolic statement of the environmental impact of the proposed design.

The traditional professional responsibilities of the
designer also need to be reconsidered. For instance, if
the designer is aware of the ecosystem implications of
the forms of energy and materials used in the built
environment and the ways in which they are used,
then he or she is obliged to be responsible for the total
ecosystem impact of the design. This implies that the

designer is responsible not only for the built system's creation and construction but also for the choice of materials and technical systems prior to its construction and the way that they are used, reused, or disposed of after its construction at the end of their physical life. Accompanying this is that considerably more research needs to be done on the ecosystem impact of the energy and material resources used in the built environment.

A system of monitoring needs to be developed so that the designer can check the ecosystem impacts of a designed system throughout its life cycle. This is a cyclical concept of architecture in which architecture cannot be regarded as completed once it is erected on site. In the ecological approach, it must be considered in the context of its entire life cycle *from source to sink*.

The term *ecological design* has previously been used very loosely to denote any approach to design which has some concern for the ecosystems, no matter how minor or remote. A more explicit explanation has not previously been provided. The following broad assumptions underlie the ecological approach to design:

- It is advantageous for people to keep their environment biologically viable.
- The present state of progressive degradation of the environment by human actions and activities is unacceptable.
- It is necessary to minimize people's destructive impacts on the ecosystems as far as possible.

Ecological design is a design process that comprehensively takes into account the adverse effects which the product of the design has on the ecosystems, and gives priority to the minimization of these adverse effects. However, before we can attempt to minimize the adverse ecosystem effects, we need to identify those aspects of the designed system which will result in these effects. We have to emphasize that in a true ecological approach, a design cannot be called ecological unless it takes into full consideration the four sets of interaction in our interactions framework.

How, then, can these concepts be implemented? A model of the conventional design process can be one that is regarded as having three main parts (Markus, 1973): *analysis, synthesis,* and *appraisal.*

1. *Analysis: defining the building program as an ecological impact statement.* This is the first stage in the design of a building. It includes the gathering of all relevant information and the establishment of relationships, constraints, objectives, and criteria, i.e., the structuring of the design problem. Martin (1966) has defined design as the establishment of a fit between the pattern of needs and use, the pattern of built form, the pattern of servicing systems, the technological factors, and the environmental factors. This is a convenient approach to the design of the built environment.

■ *The pattern of needs and use is the way in which the requirements of the users of the built system are considered and organized.* Design involves the setting down of standards of comfort (spatial and environmental) for the users of the designed system. The size and extent of spatial accommodation and the quality of environmental comfort that is provided in the designed system affect not only the ecosystem of the site on which the designed system is located but also the quantities of energy and materials (the earth's resources) that are consumed and depleted. These depend on the standard of needs and use required by the people who will use the built environment or the people who commissioned its design. The higher the levels of needs and use, the more extensive will be the size of the designed system and its subsystems, and consequently the greater will be its ecosystem impacts. An overall reduction in the environmental impacts throughout the earth can be effected if there is a similar reduction in the level of people's demand for certain needs (e.g., shelter, comfort level, mobility, food supply, etc.). Ultimately the extent of a design's impact reflects the society which commissioned it, and the further that people depart from a simple pattern of needs and use, the more complex is the support that must be derived from the environment and the more they have to plan for and expect environmental impairment. In establishing the pattern of needs and use, the following decisions would have to be made: What standard of living is required? What are users willing to give up or tolerate to have it? The ecological approach begins with the design brief and user requirements. Generally, the lower the level of requirements, the lower the impact.

- *The pattern of built form is the way in which the building spaces are massed and organized.* In the ecological approach, the built environment must be conceived as an entity consisting of not only the built system's physical substance and form, but also the operational activity which takes place within it.

We contend that the environmental impacts of the built environment are not just those inherent in the making and erection of the built elements, but include the impact that the use of these elements, their disposal, and their recovery will generate. In the ecological approach, we must analyze the designed system as an intentional intrusion into the project site's ecosystem with the purpose of finding out the extent of the changes to the ecosystem's structure and functioning caused by imposing the man-made system or activity upon the ecosystem's components.

However, because the earth is a closed materials system with a finite mass, a rational use of its ecosystems, materials, and energy resources is essential. The quantity and quality of the inputs to the built environment throughout its life cycle must be taken into account in design, and these consist of not only the energy and material resources which are used to synthesize its physical substance and form, but also those which are used to operate and maintain it in all the phases of its entire life cycle (production, construction, operation, and recovery). In the process of this life cycle, it can have considerable impact on the environment. Inherent in the use of each element of energy and material in a built system is a history of direct and indirect impacts on the earth's ecosystems and resources. At the same time, the quantity and quality of the outputs from the built environment throughout its life cycle must be taken into account in design. These consist of those exchanges of energy and materials that are discharged from the built environment into the ecosystems to be assimilated or absorbed, whether with or without some form of pretreatment.

The designer must therefore be concerned not only with the quantification of the extent and range of human needs and use of the biosphere's ecosystems and the earth's resources in the designed system (as inputs), but also with the way in which these elements are abstracted, stored, assembled, used, and finally dispersed of (or reintroduced) into the biosphere (as outputs). This pattern can be conceived in the form of the designed system's life cycle, consisting of the cyclical phases of production, construction, operation, and recovery.

In effect, we might redefine architectural design as the management of energy and materials, whereby the earth's energy and material resources (biotic and abiotic) are managed and assembled by the designer into a temporary form (viz., for the period of intended use) and then demolished at the end of this period and either recycled within the built environment or assimilated into the ecosystems. This concept has important ramifications for buildings from their inception to their eventual disposal.

The interactions framework relates and structures these aspects of the built environment with ecological consequences into four sets of interactions based on the concept of an open system. Through these, a given design can be broken down into sets of interdependent interactions with the ecological environment. These interactions are synonymous with the demands that the design makes on the ecosystems and on the earth's resources.

To summarize, the designer must consider the environmental effects that result from the following:

- *The internal-external exchanges of energy and materials,* or the impacts caused by the supply of inputs to the designed system during its life cycle.
- *The external-internal exchanges of energy and materials,* or the impacts caused by the discharges of outputs from the designed system during its life cycle.
- *The internal interdependencies of the system,* or the impacts caused by the actions and activities during the life cycle of a designed system and by the users of the designed systems.
- *The external interdependencies of the system,* or the influences of the geographical location of the designed system and its activities on the ecosystems, on other ecosystems within the biosphere, and on the earth's resources. These provide the context for the designed system.

In the same way that the ecosystem concept in ecology has provided a conceptual framework for environmental investigations, the interactions framework provides a basis for perceiving the interactions between a designed system and the ecological environment. For example, to determine the ecological consequences of a design, the designed system (or the contents of its built form) has to be broken down into its building elements and servicing systems, which we can then relate to the sets of interactions within our framework. A specific building can therefore be seen in terms of the interactions in its life cycle and their influence on the ecosystems.

The total ecological consequences of a built structure must be seen in relation to the phases of its life cycle. For each of these phases, the environmental interaction of each activity should be examined in accordance with our framework (i.e., the inputs to that activity, the outputs discharged, the spatial ecosystem impacts of the operation, and the total effect on the ecological systems). It is necessary to be aware of the interactions in each of the phases so that the overall consequences can be minimized. Alternative design solutions may be compared in terms of their impacts over their life cycles. For instance, the construction impacts of one design may be less than those of an alternative design, which, however, may have a larger operational impact. Simultaneously, the pattern of the built form must be seen not as a static pattern (as previously) but as a pattern that changes over time.

- *The pattern of the building's servicing systems.* The pattern of servicing systems are the ways in which the built environment's support systems are physically organized. These affect the operational pattern of the flow of energy and materials through the built environment. This pattern includes not only the servicing system but also the designed system's own physical form. The value scale that designers have previously used has been narrow in that it has considered only a small portion of the cause-and-effect relationships which the systems generate. Reflected in the design of every built structure is the designer's particular conception of the relation (or lack of relation) of that object to the biosphere.
- We find that much of existing design has been based on the erroneous assumption that the earth

is an infinite source of resources (i.e., raw materials, fossil fuel, land, etc.) and an infinite sink for the disposal of all the wastes generated. The relationship that presently exists is an open-ended linear relationship. This existing pattern can be described as a *linear once-through pattern*, in which resources are used at one end of the system and wastes are discharged at the other end. The designer's realm of consideration has been mainly the point of use. However, just as the application of technologies may have inadvertently exploited the biosphere, technologies could employ a fuller understanding of the ecological systems to develop ways in which people could live in a better balance with the ecological environment.

We identify here four possible design strategies for the pattern of use of energy and materials in the built form and in the servicing systems of the built form. These are once-through design, open-circuit design, closed-circuit design, and combined open/closed-circuit design. Morphologically, these are represented in Fig. 8-1.

The existing system in the man-made environment is the once-through system. Here, the resources are used, based on the assumption that there is an infinite resource base. The outputs are

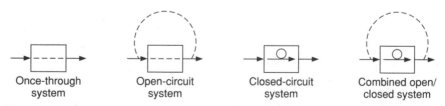

| Once-through system | Open-circuit system | Closed-circuit system | Combined open/closed system |

Figure 8-1. Patterns of use of energy and materials in the built environment.

thrown into the environment without consideration being given to their effects, the routes that they take, and their final sink.

In the open-circuit system, the design makes full use of the resilience of the environment to provide the receiving sink for the residues. Although this is similar to the once-through system, the open-circuit system stays within the limits of the assimilative abilities of the ecosystems. If this threshold is exceeded, the result will be environmental impairment. Present methods of open-circuit design involve geographical location and pretreatment processes (Holgate, 1972). For instance, industries are located in environments that are still relatively unpolluted and uncontaminated. This system makes the assumption that land resources available for such purposes are unlimited. Provided proper environmental evaluation is carried out on the location, open-circuit design is often possible in relatively unmodified locations.

In the closed-circuit system, the majority of the processes of the system are internalized. In principle, a closed-circuit design would reduce all impacts on a location to a minimum. This is true insofar as its outputs are concerned. A completely closed system is not possible, as some outputs will invariably need to be discharged. As with all living systems, if the system is to survive in the long term, then it must interact with its environment. External energy sources will still be required to maintain the internalized processes. The closed-circuit system should be used as far as possible in combination with open-circuit systems, based on a knowledge of the biophysical constraints of the ecosystems of the location.

The broad preference is that the designed systems be based on *internalized processes* insofar as possible, without having to externalize any problems on surrounding ecosystems or communities except by mutual arrangement. A combined open/closed-circuit system would reduce the environmental impacts of a once-through system, while at the same time using the assimilative abilities of the ecological environment.

These patterns represent the range of assumptions that the designer might hold regarding the relationship of the built structure to the biosphere (i.e., whether it is part of a once-through system, an open-circuit system, a closed-circuit system, or a combined open/closed-circuit system). The designer needs to design the built environment and its servicing system so that they make the least demands on the ecosystem and on the earth's resources.

- *The technological factors.*   Design is constrained by certain technological factors (e.g., availability of certain materials and forms of construction, existing technological means and their cost, present technical limitations to design invention, and availability of present techniques for data collection and evaluation). Many of the design strategies that are proposed in this study may not be justified by short-term financial returns or may be presently restricted by a scarcity of technical means. A table of the possible technological applications is shown in Fig. 8-2.

- *The environmental factors.*   These are the factors pertaining to the environment of the built form, which are influenced by the built form and in turn

Design decisions to be made	Ecological criteria to be evaluated (interactions framework)	Examples of design strategies to be considered	Examples of technological applications and inventions needed
1. Choice of building materials and construction systems	■ Depletion of energy and material resources used in that material and form of construction ■ The ecosystem impacts of that material and form of construction on the project site ■ The outputs emitted in making available that material and in the construction ■ The range of actions and activities involved in making available that material and form of construction and their impact on the ecosystems ■ Others	■ Use local source of materials ■ Design for ease of reuse in the same physical state within the built environment ■ Design for long life and multipurpose use to avoid short-term replacement ■ Design for reuse in a lower-grade form ■ Design for reuse elsewhere in the same state ■ Others	■ Demountable structures and systems to permit further reuse ■ Materials derived from renewable resources ■ Recycled materials ■ Biodegradable materials which can be assimilated into the ecosystems ■ Development of low-energy-consumption and low-pollutive forms of materials ■ Others

Figure 8-2. Strategies for ecological design.

Design decisions to be made	Ecological criteria to be evaluated (interactions framework)	Examples of design strategies to be considered	Examples of technological applications and inventions needed
2. Choice of servicing system	▪ Depletion of energy and material resources during production, construction, operation, and disposal ▪ Discharges of outputs over their life cycle ▪ Spatial impacts on the ecosystems of the project site ▪ Ecosystem impacts caused by the actions and activities over the life cycle ▪ Others	▪ Use ambient sources of energy and materials ▪ Reduce overall standard of user needs and comfort and reduce overall consumption levels ▪ Optimize use of energy and material inputs ▪ Assimilate outputs into ecosystems ▪ Recycle within the built environment ▪ Others	▪ Ambient energy sources (e.g., solar energy, wind power) ▪ More efficient technical systems ▪ Close the circuit in the systems by means of reuse and recycling systems ▪ Design systems which have a symbiotic relationship with the ecosystems ▪ Others
3. Spatial planning of built form	▪ Impacts on the ecosystem of the project site	▪ Design on a site of least ecological impact	▪ Ecosystem analysis of the site prior to location and erection

Figure 8-2. (*Continued*)

Design decisions to be made	Ecological criteria to be evaluated (interactions framework)	Examples of design strategies to be considered	Examples of technological applications and inventions needed
3. Spatial planning of built form (*cont.*)	▪ Impacts on the rehabilitation of the site after the useful life of the built form ▪ Ecological properties of the ecosystem of the project site (e.g., its assimilative ability to absorb outputs) ▪ Impacts during the life cycle of the designed system ▪ Impacts of other human actions, activities, and development encouraged by the designed system ▪ Others	▪ Eliminate the designed system from the site completely ▪ Integrate with the local pattern of landscape and ecosystem factors ▪ Respond to the properties of the local ecosystem ▪ Respond to the climatic characteristics of the location to derive a passive low-energy configuration	▪ System of monitoring of the designed system and the ecosystems

Figure 8-2. (*Continued*)

influence the operation of the built form itself. In the ecological approach, the designer must see the environment in which the designed system is to be located as more than just a spatial zone with physical, climatic, and aesthetic features. It exists as part of an ecosystem unit whose abiotic and biotic components and processes, as well as systemic properties, must be taken into account in the design. In the ecological approach, the emphasis of conventional site investigation is changed, and importance is placed upon those ecosystem properties of the project site which could influence design synthesis. The layout and location of the built system also depend upon the environmental factor. In addition to these considerations, attitudes regarding the environment as an infinite source of resources and infinite sink for wastes have to be changed to acknowledge its limitations. The designer has to be more critical of the influence of the ecosystem on the design process and the designed system.

2. *Synthesis: producing a design solution.* The interactions framework is not a substitute for design invention. Invariably, in any designed program, the designer still has to synthesize a selected set of considerations into a physical form. In this process of synthesis, the structural models described here are useful in determining the ecological interactions.

There exists at present a large body of literature (e.g., Jones, C., 1967) suggesting a variety of rational, intuitive, ordered, and random processes for design synthesis, which may be appropriate for different problems and different designers' personalities. The

process may result in a single design, a variety of
designs, or a cluster of variants of a basic type. Every
design problem represents a particular balance of the
relative importance of its principal elements and the
demands arising from each. The development in
each case of a design that is related to that balance
would appear to be an effective way of designing an
ecologically responsive built environment. Different
design methods might be viewed as alternatives
which can be used advantageously, depending on
the design problem that is being investigated. Our
intention here is not to try to determine a set of standard solutions for design (as no single solution or set
of solutions would provide an immediate correction
of all environmental problems), but to provide the
designer with insight into the aspects of environmental impairment by the built environment. In
some instances, solutions may arise that do not
require the synthesis of a physical system.

All that we can predict is the kind of design decisions and evaluations regarding the proposed
design's ecological interaction that any designer
would have to make in the process of creating the
built environment. The importance of these initial
design decisions should be stressed, for they determine the extent of initial ecosystem degradation and
affect the extent of future corrective or preventive
action.

As the final impact of a design will depend to a
large extent upon the designer's coming to grips
with the environmental interactions associated with
the design problem in the correct manner from the
start, the framework for design described here is an
approach rather than a set route. Before any design

is turned into form, the designer might make explicit maps of the problem structure using the interactions framework. These maps serve to diagram the relationships that need to be understood in order to grasp the nature of the design problem. Activities, relationships, events, and situations could be expressed graphically in a form that contains their essential attributes, then combined to show their relationships (e.g., congruent with one another, separated by a barrier, excluding an activity, etc.). These need also to be represented in a form that is generalized sufficiently so it can fit several or all concrete cases (viz., interpretations) in the real world. Such morphological analyses would emphasize fundamental differences and/or similarities rather than functional or performance features.

Our framework can be regarded as a generalized map of the problem structure. For a given design program, the interactions framework provides a way of structuring the intake so that it plays its appropriate part in determining the final design. The identification of the sets of interactions in the form of a structure provides no more than a map of the design problem. The route that the designer takes through it becomes a variable depending on the designer and the design context, provided that the designer takes into account each of the main components of the framework, the interactions within it, and the interactions between the components. Each designer or group of designers will traverse the map in a different way according to the circumstances.

3. *Appraisal: establishing the performance of the design solution.* In the conventional design process,

the appraisal stage is a retrospective act by which the designer establishes the quality of his or her solution. There are three basic steps in the conventional appraisal process (Markus, 1973):

- *Representation.* The solution is modeled in any suitable way (e.g., verbal, mathematical, visual, or even full-scale; in this sense, a building in use is a full and complete model of a design).
- *Measurement.* This is a neutral activity in which the performance of the model is determined using as wide a variety of measures as necessary (e.g., costs, environmental conditions, flexibility, space utilization, and human response).
- *Evaluation.* The measured results are evaluated using (e.g., subjective value judgments, comparison with ideal average or statutory performance standards found in the analysis, conformity to constraints recorded in the analysis, etc.).

In order to enable effective design appraisal and evaluation, further development of the interactions framework would involve appropriate quantitative data. These consist of the following (Fig. 8-3):

1. *Input criteria*
   - Quantities of energy and materials used in the designed system
   - The availability of the energy and material resources (rates of depletion)
   - The ecosystem consequences of each input used
2. *Output criteria*
   - The permissible quantities of output discharged by the designed system

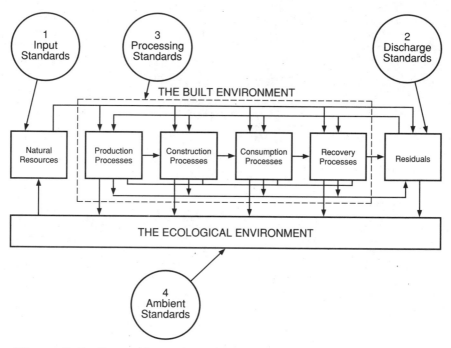

Figure 8-3. Criteria for evaluation.

- The routes taken by various outputs after discharge and their ecosystem consequences
- The energy and material cost of management of the output
- The ecosystem consequences of output management

3. *System criteria*
    - The extent of the pattern of needs and use
    - The efficiency of the system processes
    - The extent of internalization of the system processes
    - The ecosystem consequences of the realization of the designed system

The quantification of these provides no more than a statement of the extent of impacts (interactions) that a designed system has on the earth's ecosystems and the resources which need to be directed toward minimizing them. The design task becomes one of integrating the designed system's features and processes (and their functioning) with the ecosystem, with the purpose of minimizing the undesirable impacts and, through design invention, to achieve a steady-state relationship with the ecosystems (Dyson, 1992; Girardet, 1992; World Resources Institute, 1994). The fact that people alter the ecosystems by their activities need not be intrinsically undesirable or negative.

Ecological design does not imply that the entire biosphere should be preserved from human intervention entirely—say, as a nature reserve—nor is its goal to prevent all changes from taking place, since all ecosystems will change regardless of human action. Our ecological design objective is therefore not how to keep the biosphere and the ecosystems from being influenced or changed by people, but how to relate human activities to the ecosystems in the least destructive way, within the inherent limitations of the ecosystems. It should be possible in principle to design a built environment with beneficial ecological impacts. The critical design issues are how, when, and where these changes are executed.

The interactions framework does not exhaust the field of research, but it suffices, first, to define and map the ecological problems encountered in design and, second, to propose a theoretical frame of reference in which these considerations can be incorporated into the design and planning of the built environment.

An organized and directed application of ecological principles to design is still in its infancy. In many instances, much of the desired information, principles, mathematics, and problem definitions is not yet available for ready application. For example, the collection of ecological data will remain a long process because most ecological phenomena are attuned to the seasons. Ecosystem modification by building activity has been for the most part poorly understood and often unforeseen. It is essential that more attempts be made to achieve deeper understanding of environmental repercussions, to anticipate them as a regular part of design and planning, and to collect the data in a form appropriate to design analysis.

Nevertheless, this lack of absolute environmental data should not hinder the incorporation of ecological considerations into design. Although in some cases the data cannot be accurately quantified, indices should be used (e.g., water-quality index). As more empirical studies are undertaken, more accurate data should be forthcoming. Monitoring systems can be established as essential components of environmental protection systems. However, many polluting agents that are potentially detrimental have not yet been recognized as such. More reliable data are also needed on the four components of the interactions framework (i.e., the inputs of the built environment, its outputs, the life span and life cycle of its elements, and the ecological system's components and processes and their interactions with the built environment).

As mentioned earlier, the designer can design with the strategy of "buying time" until the necessary adjustments to a more ecologically responsive social consumption habit, living pattern, and value system can be made by society and the appropriate environmentally responsive technologies can be developed.

Although certain alternative technical systems have been suggested by some (Moorcraft, 1972; Wells, 1972; Baggs, 1977–1978; Morgan, 1979; etc.), these remain in the experimental stages, and further development is necessary. It has been suggested that "bionics" (the design of systems based on biological systems) may provide solutions (Yeang, 1974c). This approach is a potentially rich source for design invention (Hertel, 1966).

References

Albuquerque–Beralillio County Planning Department (1972), *Comprehensive Plan, Metropolitan Environmental Framework*, p. 52.

Alexander, C., and Manheim, M. (1962), *The Use of Diagrams in Highway Route Location: An Experiment*, Civil Engineering Systems Lab, Cambridge, MA.

Ambasz, E. (1969), "The Formation of a Design Discourse," *Perspecta: The Yale Architectural Journal*, Vol. 12.

Angyal, A. (1941), *Foundation for a Science of Personality*, Harvard University Press, Cambridge, MA.

Arvil, R. (1970), *Man and Environment*, Penguin Books, London (1st ed., 1967).

ASCE (1973), *Proceedings of the ASCE Urban Transportation Division*, "Environmental Impact" Specialty Conference (May 21–23, 1973), Chicago.

Ashby, E. (1973), "Prospect for Pollution," *Journal of the Royal Society of Arts*, June, pp. 443–453.

Ashby, F. (1971–1972), *Royal Commission on Environmental Pollution*, H.M.S.O., 1st report, 1971, 2d report, March 1972, 3d report, September 1972.

Ashby, R. (1958), *Introduction to Cybernetics*, Chapman and Hall, London.

Atkins, J., et al. (1972), *Huntington Environmental Planning Program*, University of Pennsylvania Department of Regional Planning and Landscape Architecture, M.A. thesis, Philadelphia.

Austin, R. L. (1984), *Designing the Natural Landscape*, Van Nostrand Reinhold, New York.

Ayres, R. U., and Kneese, A. U. (1969), "Production, Consumption and Externalities," *American Economic Review,* June, 59(3):282–287.

Baggs, S. A. (1977–1978), "Underground Architecture," *Architecture Australia.*

Ballard, D. W. (1974), "An American View of Problems of Materials Conservation," *Conservation of Materials,* Report of Harwell Conference, Paper 2, pp. 15–37.

Barrows, H. H. (1973), "Geography as Human Ecology," *Annals of the Association of American Geographers,* 13:1–14.

Bateson, G. (1973), *Steps to an Ecology of Mind,* Paladin, Suffolk.

Beament, J. W. L. (ed.) (1960), *Symposium of the Society for Experimental Biology,* No. 14, Cambridge University Press, Cambridge.

Beckman, I., and Weidt, E. (1973), *Archiecoframe or a Partial Analysis of the Ecological Impact of Building Materials and Residential Scale Structural Systems,* University of Minnesota Department of Architecture, Minneapolis.

Becknap, R. K., and Fartado, J. E. (1967), *Three Approaches to Environmental Resource Analysis,* Conservation Foundation, Washington, D.C.

Bender, T. (1973), *Environmental Design Primer,* Minneapolis.

Berdurski, B. L. (1973), "Ecology and Economics— Partners for Productivity," *Annals of the American Academy of Political and Social Sciences,* 410:75–94.

Benham, R. (1965), "A Home Is Not a House," *Art in America,* April.

Berry, R. (1972), "Recycling, Thermodynamics and Environmental Thrift," *Bulletin,* May.

Bertalanffy, L. von (1950), "The Theory of Open Systems in Physics and Biology," *Science,* 3:23–29.

——— (1968), *General Systems Theory,* Penguin, London.

——— and Rapoport, A. (eds.) (1956), "General

Systems," *Yearbook of the Society for the Advancement of General System Theory.*

Billings, W. D. (1964), *Plants and the Ecosystem,* Wadsworth, Belmont, CA.

Bolittho, V. (1973), "Environmental Inter-Relationships in Water Pollution Control," *Water Pollution Control.*

Bookchin, M. (1973), "Environmentalists versus Ecologists," *Undercurrents 4,* Geoffrey Boyle, London.

Borman, F. H. G., and Liken, G. E. (1967), "Nutrient Cycling," *Science,* 155:424–429.

Boughey, A. S. (1971), *Fundamental Ecology,* Interext Books, London.

Boulding, K. (1969), *Economics of the Spaceship Earth,* Harper and Row, New York.

Bowen, H. (1972), in Moorcraft, C. (ed.), "Design for Survival," *Architectural Design,* 42:418.

Bower, B. T. (1971), "Interpretation: Residuals and Environmental Management," *AIP Journal,* July, pp. 218–220.

——— et al. (1968), *Waste Management, Generation and Disposal of Solid Liquid and Gaseous Wastes in the New York Region,* A Report of the Second Regional Plan, Regional Planning Association, New York.

——— and Spofford, W. O. (1970), "Environmental Quality Management," *Natural Resources Journal,* 10(4):655–667.

Brooks, H., and Bowers, R. (1970), "The Assessment of Technology," *Scientific American,* 22:13–22.

Brown, G., and Stetlon, P. (1974), "The Energy Cost of a House," *Rational Technology Unit,* AA Publications, London.

Brown, G. Z. (1985), *Sun, Wind, and Light: Architecture Design Strategies,* Wiley, New York.

Brown, H. (1970), "Human Materials Production as a Process in the Biosphere," *Scientific American,* 223(3):194–209.

Brown, L. (1981), *Building a Sustainable Society,* Norton, New York.

————, Flavin, C., and Postel, S. (1991), *Saving the Planet*, Norton, New York.

Brubaker, S. (1972), *To Live on Earth: Man and His Environment in Perspective*, A Resources for the Future Study, Johns Hopkins Press, Baltimore.

Bural, P. (1991), *Green Design*, The Design Council, London.

Burton, I., and Kates, R. (1964), "The Perception of Natural Hazards in Resource Management," *Natural Resources Journal*, 3:412–441.

Cain, G. (1971), "The Ecological House," *Street Farmer 1*, AA Publications, London.

Cain, S. A. (1970), "The Importance of Ecological Studies as a Basis for Land Use Planning," *Biological Conservation*, Vol. 1, London.

Carr, M. (ed.) (1985), *The Appropriate Technology Reader*, Intermediate Technology Publications, London.

Carson, R. (1962), *Silent Spring*, Houghton Mifflin, Boston.

Celedrovsky, G. (1970), "Systems in Balance," Office of Architecture and Planning, March.

Chanlett, E. T. (1973), *Environmental Protection*, McGraw-Hill, New York.

Chapman, P. (1973), "The Energy Cost of Producing Copper and Aluminum from Primary Sources," Open University Report ERG 001, United Kingdom; and in *Metals and Materials*, February, pp. 107–111.

Chappell, C. L. (1973), "Disposal Technology for Hazardous Wastes," *Surveyor*, November 2, pp. 501–502.

Charney, M. (1969), "Environmental Strategies: Notes for Environmental Design," *Perspecta: The Yale Architectural Journal*, Vol. 12.

Chermayeff, S., and Tzonis, A. (1971), *Shape of Community (Realisation of Human Potential)*, Penguin Books, London.

Ciriary-Wantrup, S. V., and Parsons, J. V. (eds.) (1967), *Natural Resources: Quality and Papers Presented at*

Faculty Seminars (1961–1965), University of California Press, Berkeley.

Clarke, R. (1972), "Soft Technology: Blueprint for a Research Community," *Undercurrents,* No. 2, May.

Clements, F. E. (1946), *Plant Succession: An Analysis of the Development of Vegetation*, Carnegie Institute, Wachsman Publishers, pp. 242, 515.

Cole, LaMont C. (1958), "The Ecosphere," *Scientific American.*

Collingwood, R. G. (1945), *The Idea of Nature*, Clarendon Press, Oxford.

Colinvaux, Paul R. (1973), "The Ecosystem as a Practical Model," *Introduction to Ecology*, Wiley, New York, pp. 229–245.

Common, M. (1973), "Economics and the Environmental Problem," discussion papers in *Conservation*, No. 5, University College, London.

Commoner, B. (1971), *The Closing Circle: Confronting the Environmental Crisis*, Jonathan Cape, London.

Cook, E. (1971), "The Flow of Energy in an Industrial Society," *Scientific American*, 224(3):134–147.

Cooke, G. D., et al. (1968), "The Case for the Multi-species Ecological System with Special Reference to Succession and Stability," *Biogenerative Systems*, NADA Spec. 165, pp. 129–130.

Costin, A. B. (1959), "Replaceable and Irreplaceable Resources and Land Use," *Journal of the American Institute of Agricultural Science*, March, pp. 3–9.

Crosby, T. (1973), *The Environmental Game*, Penguin, London.

Cumberland, J. H. (1966), "A Regional Inter-Industry Model for Analysis of Development Objectives," *Regional Science Association Papers*, 17:68.

Dales, J. H. (1968), *Pollution, Property and Prices: An Essay in Policy Making and Economics*, University of Toronto Press, Toronto.

Daly, H. (1991), *Steady-State Economics*, Island Press, Washington, D.C.

Dasman, R. F. (1968), *Environmental Conservation*, Wiley, New York.

———— (1972), "Towards a System for Classifying Natural Regions of the World and Their Representation by National Parks and Reserves," *Biological Conservation*, 4:247–255.

————, Milton, J. P., and Freeman, P. H. (1973), *Ecological Principles for Economic Development*, Wiley, London.

Davoll, J. (1971), Statement to the Conservation Society by the Minister of the Environment on the U.N. Stockholm 1972 Conference, London.

Dee, N., Whitman, I. L., McGinnis, J. T., and Fahringer, D. C. (1971), *Design of an Environmental Evaluation System*, Bureau of Reclamation, U.S. Department of the Interior, 14-06-D-7005, Battelle Memorial Institute Publication, Columbus, OH.

Detwyler, T. R. (1971), *Man's Input of the Environment*, McGraw-Hill, New York.

———— and Marcus, M. G. (eds.) (1972), *Urbanization and Environment*, Duxbury Press, Belmont, CA.

Dewey, J. (1929), *Experience and Nature*, Open Court, La Salle, IL.

Diamont, R. M. E. (1971), "The Prevention of Pollution," *Heating and Ventilation Engineer*.

Dickson, D. (1974), *Alternative Technology and the Politics of Technical Change*, Fontana, London.

Dubin, F. S., et al. (1974), *Energy Conservation Design Guidelines for Office Buildings*, report for General Services Administration/Public Building Service.

Dubos, R. J. (1967), "Man Adapting: His Limitation and Potentialities," in Ewald, W. R., Jr. (ed.), *Environment for Man: The Next 50 Years*, Indiana University Press, Bloomington.

Duffey, E., and Watt, A. S. (eds.) (1970), *The Scientific Management of Animal and Plant Communities for*

Conservation, 11th Symposium of the British Ecological Society, University of East Anglia, Norwich, July 7–9, Blackwell, London.

Dunn, J. B., and Hington, J. A. (1970), *The Re-Vegetation of Despoiled Land*, Public Works and Municipal Services Congress, No. 14, Oyez Press, London.

Dunn, P. D. (1978), *Appropriate Technology: Technology with a Human Face*, Macmillan, London.

Durrell, L. (1986), *GAA State of the Ark Atlas*, Doubleday, New York.

Dyson, F. (1992), *From Eros to Gaia*, Penguin Books, London.

Egler, F. E. (1972), "Vegetation as an Object of Study," *Philosophy of Science*, 9(3):245–260.

Ehrenfield, O. W. (1970), *Biological Conservation*, Holt, Rinehart & Winston, New York.

Ehrlich, P. R., and Ehrlich, A. H. (1970), *Population, Resources, Environment: Essay in Human Ecology*, W. H. Druman, San Francisco.

Ellul, J. (1965), *The Technological Society*, Knopf, New York.

Elton, C. S. (1968), *The Ecology of Invasions by Animals and Plants*, Chapman and Hall, London.

Emery, F. E. (ed.) (1969), *Systems Thinking*, Penguin, London, pp. 241–260.

Emery, F. E., and Trist, E. C. (1965), "The Causal Textures of Organisational Environments," *Human Relations*, 18:21–32.

Engensberger, H. M. (1974), "A Critique of Political Society," *New Left Review*, 84, Building and Mansell, London, pp. 3–31.

Evans, F. C. (1951), "Biology and Urban Areal Research," *The Scientific Monthly*, 73:37–38.

—— (1956), "Ecosystems as the Basic Unit in Ecology," *Science*, 123:1127–1128.

Fathy, H. (1986), *Natural Energy and Vernacular Architecture*, University of Chicago Press, Chicago.

Flajser, S. H., and Porter, A. C. (1974), "Towards a

Science for Technology Assessment," *The Trend in Engineering,* 25(2), College of Engineering, University of Washington.

Flavin, C. (1986), *Energy and Architecture: The Solar and Conservation Potential,* Worldwatch Institute, Washington, D.C.

Flawn, P. T. (1970), *Environmental Geology,* Harper and Row, New York.

Fox, A., and Murrell, R. (1989), *Green Design,* Architecture Design and Technology Press, London.

Fraser, D. F. (1969), *Wilderness and Plants,* Reith Lectures, BBC.

—————— and Dasman, R. F. (1972), "The Ecosystem View of Human Society," *Realities,* June.

—————— and Milton, J. P. (eds.) (1966), *Future Environments of North America,* The Natural History Press, Garden City, NY.

Fuller, B. (1952), "The Autonomous Dwelling Facility," *Perspecta: The Yale Architectural Journal,* Summer.

—————— et al. (1963), *World Design Science Decade 1965–1975,* Southern Illinois University Press, Carbondale, IL.

Gabel, M. (1975), *Energy, Earth & Everyone,* Simon and Schuster, New York.

Geiger, T. (1971), *The Climate Near the Ground,* MIT Press, Cambridge, MA.

Gerardin, L. (1968), *Bionics,* World University Library, New York.

Girardet, H. (1992), *The Gaia Atlas of Cities,* Gaia Books Ltd., London.

Glickson, A. (1953), *Regional Planning and Development,* Leiden A.W., Sijthoff's Nitgerensmaatschaffij, N.V., six lectures at Institute of Social Studies, The Hague.

Goldsmith, E. (1970), "Limits of Growth in Natural Systems," *General Systems,* 15.

—————— (1971), *Can Britain Survive?* Sphere Books Ltd., London.

Gordon, A. (1972), "The President Introduces His Long Life/Loose Fit/Low Energy Study," *RIBAJ*, September, pp. 374–375.

Graham, E. (1944), *Natural Principles of Land Use*, Oxford University Press, Oxford.

Grant, D. P., and Ward, W. S. (1970), "A Computer-Aided Space Allocation Technique," *Kentucky Workshop on Computer Applications to Environmental Design*, Lexington, KY.

GSA (1974), *Energy Conservation Design Guidelines for Office Building*, prepared by Dublin-Mindell-Bloome Associates in cooperation with AA Research Group.

Hackett, B. (1966), "Ecological Principles and Landscape Planning," *Towards a New Relationship of Man and Nature in Temperate Lands*, UNESCO, IUCN, No. 8, June.

Hall, A. D., and Fraser, R. E. (1966), "Definition of Systems," *General Systems*, 1:18–28.

Halphin, L., et al. (1966), "Ecological Architecture: Planning the Organic Environment," *Progressive Architecture*, May, pp. 120–137.

Hamilton, D. (1971), *Technology, Man and the Environment*, Faber and Faber, London, p. 211.

Hammon, B. (1973), *System Energy and Recycling: A Study of the Beverage Industry*, CAC 23, Center for Advanced Computation, University of Illinois, Urbana, March 17.

Harper, P. (1974), "What's Left of Alternative Technology?," *Undercurrents*, 6:35–39.

Harte, J., and Socolow, R. H. (1971), *Patient Earth*, Holt, Rinehart & Winston, New York.

Hasler, A. D., et al. (eds.) (1972), *Man in the Living Environment*, Report on the Workshop of Global Ecological Problems (1971), The Institute of Ecology, University of Wisconsin Press, Madison.

Hayhow, D. (1974), *Materials in Building Circles*, dissertation presented for the second Diploma Examination, University School of Architecture, Cambridge.

Hertel, H. (1966), *Structure, Form and Movement: Biology and Technology*, Van Nostrand Reinhold, New York.

Hey, R. W., and Perrin, R. M. S. (1960), *The Geology and Soils of Cambridgeshire*, Cambridge Natural History Society.

Hillier, B. (1977), "Architectural Research: A State of Mind," *RIBAJ*, May, p. 202.

Hirst, E. (1973), *Energy Implications of Several Environmental Quality Strategies*, ORNL-NSF-EP-53, Oak Ridge National Laboratory, Tennessee.

Holdren, J. P., and Ehrlich, P. R. (1974), "Human Population and the Global Environment," *American Scientist*, 62:282–292.

Holgate, M. W. (1972), *Action Against Pollution*, Central Unit on Environmental Pollution, D.O.E.

Holling, C. S., and Golberg, M. A. (1971), "Ecology and Planning," *AIPJ*, July, pp. 221–230.

——— (1973), "The Nature and Behaviour of Ecological Systems," in *An Anthology of Selected Readings for the National Conference on Managing the Environment*, Int. City Management Association, Washington, D.C., pp. 1–21.

——— and Gordon, O. (1971), "Towards an Urban Ecology," *Bulletin of the Ecological Society of America*, June.

Hough, M. (1984), *City Form and Natural Process*, Routledge, London.

Hughes, M. K. (1974), "The Urban Ecosystem," *Biologist*, 21(3):117–127.

Hutchinson, J. (1974), "Land Restoration in Britain—by Nature and Man," *Environmental Conservation*, 1(1):37–41.

Institute of Ecology (1972), *Man in the Living Environment*, University of Wisconsin Press, Madison.

Isard, W., et al. (1969), "On the Linkage of Socio-Economic and Ecologic Systems," *The Regional Sciences Association Papers*, 21:79–99.

Isola, A. V. D. (1973), "New Concepts of Construction Costs," *Actual Specifying Engineer,* June, p. 116.

Istock, C. A. (1971), "Modern Environmental Deterioration as a Natural Process," *International Journal of Environmental Studies,* 1:151–155.

——— (1973), "Some Ecological Criteria for the Preparation and Review of Environmental Impact Statements," *Proceedings of the ASCE Urban Transportation Division*, "Environmental Impact Statements," Specialty Conference (May 21–23, 1973), Chicago.

——— (1974), personal communication.

Jeger, L. (1970), *Taken for Granted,* HMSO, London.

Jones, C. (1967), *Design Methods,* Wiley-Interscience, New York.

Jones, M. V. (1971), *A Technology Assessment Methodology: Some Basic Propositions,* prepared in cooperation with and for the office of Science and Technology, Executive Office of the President, Washington, The Mitre Corporation, MTR-6009, Vol. 1, NTIS PB 202778-01.

Kahn, H. (1978), *The Next 200 Years,* Abacus, London.

Kaiser, E. J., et al. (1974), *Promoting Environmental Quality Through Urban Planning and Controls,* U.S. Environmental Protection Agency, Socio-Economic Environmental Studies Division, EPA-600/5/-73-015.

Kasabor, G. (1979), "The Key to Energy Conservation," *RIBAJ,* October.

Keeble, L. (1952), *Principles of Town and Country Planning,* Estates Gayette Ltd., London.

Klaff, J. L. (1973), "Necessary to Conserve U.S. Resources," *Environmental Science and Technology,* 7(10):913–916.

Kneese, A. V., Rolfe, S. E., and Harned, J. W. (eds.) (1971), *Managing the Environment: International Cooperation for Pollution Control,* Praeger, New York.

Knowles, R. C. (1974), *Energy and Form: An Ecological Approach to Urban Growth,* MIT Press, Cambridge, MA.

Koenig, H., Cooper, W., and Fahrey, J. M. (1971), "The

Industrial Ecosystem," *Our Technological Environment: Challenge and Opportunity,* American Society for Engineering Education, Industrial Engineering Education Services, January 28–29, Arizona State University, pp. 1–4.

Konecci, E. B. (1964), "Space Ecological Systems," in Schaefer, R. E. (ed.), *Bioastronautics,* New York, pp. 274–304.

———— and Wood, N. E. (1969), "Design of an Operational Ecological System," *Proceedings of the Manned Space Symposium,* Institute of the Aeronautical Sciences, April 20–22, pp. 137–150.

Kormondy, E. J. (1969), *Concepts of Ecology,* Prentice-Hall, Englewood Cliffs, NJ.

Krebs, C. J. (1972), *Ecology: The Experimental Analysis of Distribution and Abundance,* Harper and Row, New York.

Landers, R. R. (1969), *Man's Place in the Dybiosphere,* Prentice-Hall, Englewood Cliffs, NJ.

LaPorte, C. F., et al. (1972), *The Earth and Human Affairs,* Committee on Geological Sciences, Division of Earth Sciences, ARC-NAS, Canfield Press, San Francisco.

Leontief, W. (1970), "Economic Repercussions and the Economic Structure: An Input-Output Approach," *Review of Economics and Statistics,* 52:262–271.

Leopold, A. (1949), *A Land County Almanac,* Oxford University Press, London.

Leopold, L. B., Clarke, F. E., Harshaw, B. B., and Balsey, J. R. (1971), *A Procedure for Evaluating Environmental Impact,* Geological Survey Circular No. 645, U.S. Geological Survey, Washington, D.C.

Lewis, P. H. (1967a), *Study of Recreation and Open Space in Illinois,* University of Pennsylvania Department of Regional Planning and Landscape Architecture Report.

———— (1967b), *Regional Design for Human Impact,* Upper Mississippi River Comprehensive Basin Study, UMRB

Coordinating Council, Thomas Kankauna Printing and Publishing, Wisconsin.

Linton, R., et al. (1967), *A Strategy for Livable Environments*, The Task Force on Environmental Health and Related Problems, U.S. Department of Health, Education and Welfare, Washington, D.C.

Lovejoy, D. (1973), "The Need for Landscape Planning," RTPI/ILA one-day seminar, November 21, Nottingham.

Lovins, A. B. (1977), *Soft Energy Paths*, Penguin, London.

MAB (1972), *Expert Panel on the Rule of Systems Analysis and Modelling Approaches in the Man and Biosphere Programmes*, April 18–20, Paris.

Makhijani, A. B., and Lichtenberg, A. J. (1972), "Energy and Well-Being," *Environment*, Vol. 14, No. 15.

Margalef, F. (1963), "On Certain Unifying Principles in Ecology," *The American Naturalist*, 97(897):357.

Markus, T. (1973), in *Value in Building*, Elsevier, London.

Marquis, S. (1968), "Ecosystems, Societies and Cities," *American Bahavioural Scientist*, July–August, pp. 11–15.

Martin, L. (1966), "Architects' Approach to Architecture," *RIBAJ*, May.

Maser, C. (1988), *The Redesigned Forest*, R & E Miles, San Pedro, CA.

Matthews, W. H., Smith, F. E., and Golberg, E. D. (eds.) (1971), *Man's Impact on Terrestrial and Oceanic Ecosystems*, MIT Press, Cambridge, MA.

McDonough, W. (1992), *The Hannover Principles: Design for Sustainability*, William McDonough Architects, New York.

McHale, J. (1967), "World Dwelling," *Perspecta: The Yale Architectural Journal*, 11:211–230.

——— (1972), *The Ecological Context*, Collier-MacMillan, New York.

McHarg, I. (1966), "Ecological Determinism," in Darling, F. F., and Milton, J. P. (eds.), *Future Environments of North America*, Natural History Press, Garden City, NY, pp. 526–538.

———— (1968), "Ecology for the Evolution of Planning and Design," *VIA 1, Ecology in Design*.

———— et al. (1969a), *An Ecological Study of the Twin Cities Metropolitan Area,* Final Report, prepared for the Metropolitan Council of the Twin Cities.

———— (1969b), *Design with Nature,* Doubleday, Natural History Press, Garden City, NY.

———— and Berger, H. (1973), *Hazleton: An Ecological Planning Study,* University of Pennsylvania Department of Regional Planning and Landscape Architecture Report.

———— et al. (1971), *Amelia Island, Florida: A Report on the Master Planning Process for a New Recreational Community,* University of Pennsylvania Department of Regional Planning and Landscape Architecture Report.

———— et al. (1973), *Pardisan: Park in Tehran,* A Feasibility Study for an Environmental Park in Tehran, Iran, for the Imperial Government of Iran.

McIntosh, R. P. (1963), "Ecosystem, Evolution and Relational Patterns of Living Organisms," *American Scientist,* 51:246–267.

McKibben, B. (1989), *The End of Nature,* Random House, New York.

McKillop, A. (1972), Poster for Low Impact Technology.

Meadows, D. H., Meadows, D. L., Randers, J., and Behrens, W. W. (1972), *The Limits to Growth: Potomac,* Earth Island, London.

Mellanby, K. (1972), *The Biology of Pollution,* Edward Arnold, London.

Miller, J. G. (1965), "Living Systems: Basic Concepts," *Behavioural Science,* October, pp. 193–237.

Miller, R. E. (1966), "Interregional Feedback Effects in Input-Output Models: Some Preliminary Results," *Papers and Procedures of the Regional Services Association,* 17:105–125.

Moorcraft, C. (ed.) (1972), "Design for Survival," *Architectural Design*, Vol. 42, July.

——— (1973), "Some Proposals for the Reserving of an Urban Terrace House," *Street Framers.*

Morgan, W. (1979), "Earth Architecture," *Progressive Architecture*, April.

Morris, P. (1961), *Homes for Today and Tomorrow*, HMSO, London.

Morrison, W. I. (1972), "The Development of an Urban Interindustry Model: 1. Building the Input-Output Account," *Environment and Planning*, 5:369–385.

Nagel, S. (1961), *The Structure of Science, Problems in the Logic of Scientific Explanation*, Routledge & Kegan, London.

NAS-NRC Committee on Pollution (1966), *Waste Management and Control*, Publication No. 1400 NAS-NRC, Washington, D.C.

National Academy of Sciences (1990), *One Earth, One Future*, National Academy Press, Washington, D.C.

Newbold, P. J. (1964), "Production Ecology and the International Biological Programme," *Geography*, 49:98–104.

Nichosan, M. (1970), *The Environmental Revolution*, Hodder and Stoughton, London.

Norton, G. A., and Parlour, J. W. (1972), "The Economic Philosophy of Pollution: A Critique," *Environment and Planning*, 4:3–11.

Odum, E. P. (1962), "Relationship between Structure and Function in the Ecosystem," *Journal of Ecology*, 12:108–118.

——— (1963), *Ecology*, Holt, Rinehart & Winston, New York.

——— (1968), "Energy Flow in Ecosystems: A Historical Review," *American Zoology*, 8:11–18.

——— (1969), "The Strategy of Ecosystem Development," *Science*, 164:262–270.

———— (1971), *Fundamentals of Ecology*, W. B. Saunders & Co., Philadelphia.

———— (1972), "Ecosystems," in White, W., and Little, F. J. (eds.), *Essays on Ecology and Pollution*, North American Publishing Company, Philadelphia, pp. 66–69.

Odum, H. T. (1963), "Limits of Remote Ecosystems Containing Man," *American Biology Teacher*, October, pp. 429–443.

———— (1971), *Environment, Power and Society*, Wiley-Interscience, New York.

———— (1972), "An Energy Circuit Language for Ecological and Social Systems at Physical Basis," in Pattern, B. C. (ed.), *System Analysis and Simulations in Ecology*, Vol. 2, Academic Press, New York.

———— and Peterson, L. L. (1972), "Relationship of Energy and Complexity in Planning," *Architectural Design*, October, pp. 624–628.

Ogburn, C. (1970), "Where the Food Is to Come From," *Population Bulletin*, Population Reference Bureau Inc., Washington, D.C., June 2, p. 8.

O'Riorden, T. (1971), *Perspectives on Resource Management*, Pion Ltd., London.

Ortega, A., Rybezynoki, W., Ayord, S., Ali, W., and Acheson, A. (1972), *The Ecol Operation: The Problem Is No. 2*, Minimum Housing Group, School of Architecture, McGill University, Montreal, Canada.

Ovington, J. D. (1964), "The Ecological Basis of the Management of Woodland Nature Reserves in Great Britain," *Journal of Ecology*, 52 (Suppl.):29–37.

Papanek, V. (1985), *Design for the Real World: Human Ecology and Social Change*, Academy Chicago Publishers, Chicago.

Patterson, W. C. (1990), *The Energy Alternative*, McDonald & Co., London.

Pawley, M. (1974), "The Cambridge Autonomous House," *Building Design*, November.

Pearson, D. (1989), *The Natural House Book*, Simon and Schuster, New York.

Peranio, A. (1973), *The Environmental Crisis—A Cybernetic Challenge*, Technion, Israel Institute of Technology, Haifa, Israel, p. 122.

Philips, J. (1934), "Succession, Development, the Climax and the Complex Organism: An Analysis of Concepts," *Journal of Ecology*, 22:554–571.

——— (1968), "Ecology and the Ecological Approach," in *VIA 1, Ecology and Design*, University of Pennsylvania.

Pielou, E. C. (1969), *An Introduction to Mathematical Ecology*, Wiley-Interscience, New York.

Plass, G. N. (1969), "Carbon Dioxide and Climate," *Scientific American*, July, p. 6.

Poore, M. E. D. (1972), "Ecology and Conservation in Landuse," *Chartered Surveyor*, November.

Ramphal, S. (1992), *Our Country, the Planet*, Island Press, Washington, D.C.

Ray, C. (1970), "Ecology, Law and the Marine Revolution," *Biological Conservation*, Vol. 3, No. 1.

Redding, M. J. (1973), *Aesthetics in Environmental Planning*, EPA-60015-73-009, Environmental Protection Agency Office of Research and Development, U.S. Government Printing Office, Washington, D.C.

Ripley, S. D., and Buechner, H. K. (1967), "Ecosystem Science as a Point of Synthesis," *Daedalus*, 96:1192–1199.

Roaf, S., and Hancock, M. (eds.) (1992), *Energy Efficient Building*, Wiley, New York.

Roberts, D. G. M. (1972), "Public Health Engineering in the External Environment: Water Supply and Reuse, Waste Disposal and Pollution Control," *Phil. Trans. Royal Soc. London*, A 272:639–650.

Rosen, H. J. (1973), "Energy Crisis and Materials," *Progressive Architecture*, 12:76.

Rowe, J. S. (1961), "The Level-of-Integration Concept and Ecology," *Ecology*, 42:420–427.

Sagasti, F. (1970), "A Conceptual and Taxonomic

Framework for the Analysis of Adaptive Behaviour," in *General Systems Yearbook*, 15:151–160.

Salem, O. S. (1990), "Toward Sustainable Architecture and Urban Design: Categories, Methodologies and Models," unpublished manuscript, Rensselaer Polytechnic Institute, Troy, NY.

Schultz, A. M. (1969), "A Study of an Ecosystem: The Arctic Tundra," in Van Dyne, G. M. (ed.), *The Ecosystem Concept in Natural Resources Management*, Academic Press, New York, pp. 77–93.

Sears, P. B. (1956), "The Process of Environmental Change by Man," in Thomas, W. L. (ed.), *Man's Role in Changing the Face of the Earth*, University of Chicago Press, Chicago, pp. 471–484.

Seborg, G. T. (1969), "The Environment and What to Do about It," *Nuclear News*, July.

Seddan, J. W. (1973), *A Proposal to the National Endowment for the Arts for Support of a Project in Environmental Design*, mimeographed.

Sharkawy, M. A., and Graaskamp, J. A. (1971), *Inland Lakes Renewal and Management Demonstration*, Environmental Awareness Center, School of Natural Resources, University of Wisconsin.

Shiva, V. (1993), *Biodiversity: A Third World Perspective*, Third World Network, Malaysia.

Simon, H. A. (1969), *The Sciences of the Artificial*, MIT Press, Cambridge, MA.

Simonds, J. O. (1978), *Earthscape: A Manual of Environmental Planning*, McGraw-Hill, New York.

Simpson, E. H. (1949), "Measurement of Diversity," *Nature*, 163:688.

Sjors, H. (1955), "Remarks on Ecosystems," in *Svensk Batanisk Tidskrift*, Bd. 49, H 1–2.

Skinner, B. (1969), *Earth Resources*, Prentice-Hall, Englewood Cliffs, NJ.

S.M.I.C. (1970), *Inadvertent Climate Modification: Report of the Study of Man's Impact on Climate (SMIC)*, MIT Press, Cambridge, MA.

Smith, D. R. (1971), "Pollution and Range Ecosystems," in Matthews, W. H., Smith, F. E., and Golberg, E. D. (eds.), *Man's Impact on Terrestrial and Oceanic Ecosystems*, MIT Press, Cambridge, MA.

Sorenson, J. C. (1972), "Some Procedures and Programs for Environmental Impact Assessment," in Ditton, R. B., and Goodale, T. L. (eds.), *Environmental Impact Philosophy and Methods*, Proceedings of the Conference on Environmental Impact Analysis, Green Bay, WI (January 4–5), Sea Grant Publishing, WIS-SG-72-111, pp. 97–106.

———— and Moss, M. L. (1973), *Procedures and Programs to Assist in the Environmental Impact Statement Process*, University of California/University of Southern California, SG-PUB-No. 27, USC-SG-AS2-73.

———— and Pepper, J. E. (1973), *Procedures for Regional Clearinghouse Review of Environmental Impact Statements—Phase Two*, Association of Bay Area Governments (ABAG) Report No. 1010-1.4, April, draft.

Spofford, W. O. (1971), "Residuals Management," in Matthews, W. H., Smith, F. E., and Golberg, E. D. (eds.), *Man's Impact on Terrestrial and Oceanic Ecosystems*, MIT Press, Cambridge, MA, pp. 477–488.

———— (1973), "Total Environmental Management Models," in Deininger, R. A. (ed.), *Models for Environmental Pollution Control*, Ann Arbor Scientific Publications, Ann Arbor, Michigan.

St. John, A. (ed.) (1992), *The Sourcebook for Sustainable Design*, Architects for Social Responsibility, Boston Society of Architects.

Stamp, D. (1969), *Nature Conservation in Great Britain*, Collins, London.

Stoddart, D. R. (1967), "Organism and Ecosystem as Geographical Models," in Charley, R., and Haggert, P. (eds.), *Models in Geography*, Methuen and Co., London.

Szezelkun, S. A. (1973), "Energy," *Survival Scrapbook 5,* Unicon Books, Brighton/Seattle.

Tansley, A. G. (1935), "The Use and Abuse of Vegetational Concepts and Terms," *Ecology,* 16:(3).

Taylor, P. (1986), *Respect for Nature,* Princeton University Press, Princeton.

Tearle, K. (ed.) (1973), *Industrial Pollution Control: The Practical Implications,* Business Books, London.

Tebbutt, T. H. Y. (1971), *Principles of Water Pollution Control,* Pergammon Press, Oxford.

Thring, J. B. (1973), *The Autonomous House Project,* Technical Research Division Brochure, Department of Architecture, University of Cambridge.

Todd, N. J., and Todd, J. (1984), *Bioshelters, Ocean Arks, City Farming: Ecology as the Basis of Design,* Sierra Club Books, San Francisco.

Toftner, R. O. (1973), "A Balance Sheet for the Environment," *Planning,* the ASPO (American Society of Planning Officers) Magazine, July.

Tolman, E. C., and Brunswick, E. (1935), "The Organism and the Causal Texture of the Environment," *Psychological Review,* 42:43–77.

Tubbs, C. R., and Blackwood, J. W. (1971), "Ecological Evaluation of Land for Planning Purposes," *Biological Conservation,* 3(3):169–172.

Tukey, J. W., et al. (Environmental Pollution Panel, President's Science Advisory Committee) (1965), *Restoring the Quality of the Environment,* U.S. Government Printing Office, Washington, D.C.

Turk, A., Turk, J., and Wittes, J. (1972), *Ecology Pollution Environment,* W. B. Saunders, Philadelphia.

U.S.D.H. (U.S. Department of Health) (1968), *1968 National Survey of Community Solid Waste Practices,* U.S. Department of Health, Education, and Welfare, Environmental Control Administration.

Vale, B. (1972), *The Autonomous House,* Technical

Research Division Publications, Department of Architecture, University of Cambridge.

Vale, B., and Vale, R. (1991a), *Towards a Green Architecture*, RIBA Publications, London.

—— (1991b), *Green Architecture*, Thames & Hudson, London.

Van der Ryn, S., and Calthorpe, P. (1986), *Sustainable Communities*, Sierra Club Books, San Francisco.

Van Dyne, G. M. (1966), *Ecosystems, Systems Ecology and Systems Ecologists*, ORNL-3957, Oak Ridge National Laboratory, Tennessee.

—— (ed.) (1969), *The Ecosystem Concept in Natural Resource Management*, Academic Press, New York.

Victor, P. A. (1972), *Pollution: Economy and Environment*, George Allen and Unwin Ltd., London.

Villeco, M. (ed.) (1974), *Energy Conservation in Building Design, A Report to the Ford Foundation Energy Policy Project*, AIA Research Corporation, Washington, D.C.

Waggoner, P. E. (1966), "Weather Modification and the Living Environment," in Fraser, D. F., and Milton, J. E. (ed.) (1966), *Future Environments of North America*, The Natural History Press, Garden City, NY.

Walmsley, D. J. (1972), *Systems Theory: A Framework for Human Geographical Enquiry*, Research School of Pacific Studies, Australian National University, ANU Press, Canberra.

Walton, K. (1973), *The Problem of Developmental Impacts on the Countryside*, Department of Geography, University of Aberdeen.

Wann, D. (1990), *Biologic: Environmental Protection by Design*, Johnson Books, Boulder, p. 206.

World Resources Institute (1994), *The 1994 Environmental Almanac*, Houghton Mifflin, Boston.

Wott, K. E. F. (1968), *Ecology and Resource Management*, McGraw-Hill, New York.

Weddle, A. E., and Pickard, J. (1969), "Techniques in

Landscape Evaluation," in *Journal of the Town Planning Institute*, Vol. 55, No. 9.

Wells, M. B. (1971), *The Great Ecologic Colouring Book of Life and Death and Architecture*, The Conservation Account, Cherry Hill, NJ.

Wells, M. B. (1972), "An Ecologically Sound Architecture Is Possible," *Architectural Design*, 7:433.

Wells, M. (1982), *Gentle Architecture*, McGraw-Hill, New York.

Welmer, A. D., and Hoyt, H. (1966), *Real Estate*, Ronald Press Co., New York, p. 74.

Wettqvst, O. F., et al. (1971), *Identification and Evaluation of Coastal Resource Patterns in Florida*, Florida Coastal Coordination Council.

White, G. F. (1972), "Environmental Impact Statements," *The Professional Geographer*, 24(4):302–309.

Whittaker, R. H. (1953), "A Consideration of Climax Theory: The Climax as a Population and Pattern," *Ecological Monographs*, 23(1):41–78.

Wilen, J. E. (1973), "A Model of Economic System— Ecosystem Interaction," *Environment and Planning*, 5:409–420.

Willard, B. E., and Marr, J. W. (1970), "Effects of Human Activities on Alpine Tundra Ecosystem in Rocky Mountain National Park, Colorado," *Biological Conservation*, Vol. 2, No. 2.

Williams, E. R., and House, P. W. (1974), *The State of the System Model (SOS): Measuring Growth Concepts Using Ecological Concepts*, EPA-600/5-73-013, U.S. Environmental Protection Agency, Socio-Economic Environmental Studies Series, Office of Research and Development, U.S. Government Printing Office, Washington, D.C.

Windheim, L. S. (1973), "A System Morphology for Examining Energy Utilisation in Buildings," in *Journal of the BRAB Building Research Institute*, NAS July/December, pp. 1–6.

Wolman, A. (1965), *Scientific American Book on Cities,* Penguin, London.

Woodwell, G. M. (1971), "Effects on Pollution on the Structure and Physiology of Ecosystems," in Matthew, W. H., Smith, F. E., and Golberg, E. D. (eds.) (1971), *Man's Impact on Terrestrial and Oceanic Ecosystems,* MIT Press, Cambridge, MA, pp. 47–58.

—— and Hall, C. A. S. (1972), "The Ecological Effects of Energy: A Basis for Policy in Regional Planning," in *Energy, Environment and Planning the Long Island Sound Region,* Proceedings of the Conference at Brookhaven National Laboratory, BNL-50355, October 12.

Yeang, K. (1972), "Bases for Ecosystem Design," *Architectural Design,* July, pp. 434–436.

—— (1974a), *Whole Earth Energy and Materials Catalogue,* AA Publications for Unit 5, London.

—— (1974b), "Energetics of the Built Environment," *Architectural Design,* July.

—— (1974c), "Bionics—The Use of Biological Analogies in Design," *Architectural Association Quarterly (AAQ),* 4:48–57.

Zwicky, F. (1957), *Morphological Astronomy,* Springer-Verlag, Berlin.

—— (1967), "The Morphological Approach to Discovery, Invention, Research and Construction," in Zwicky, F., and Wilson, A. G. (eds.), *New Methods of Thought and Procedure,* Springer-Verlag, New York.

Index

About the Author

Ken Yeang is principal and partner of the architectural firm of T. R. Hamzah & Yeang Sendirian Berhad. His work has been featured in many international journals, including *Architectural Record* and *Progressive Architecture*. Dr. Yeang holds a doctoral degree in architecture from Cambridge University, where he specialized in environmental issues applied to building design.